Revolutionary
Rapid
Training
Method

WATER
DOG

by

RICHARD A.
WOLTERS

Author of GUN DOG, GAME
DOG, and FAMILY
DOG

Introduction by
Art Smith
Outdoor Editor NEW YORK HERALD TRIBUNE

DUTTON

DUTTON
Published by the Penguin Group
Penguin Books USA Inc., 375 Hudson Street, New York, New York
10014, U.S.A.
Penguin Books Ltd, 27 Wrights Lane, London W8 5TZ, England
Penguin Books Australia Ltd, Ringwood, Victoria, Australia
Penguin Books Canada Ltd, 10 Alcorn Avenue, Toronto, Ontario,
Canada M4V 3B2
Penguin Books (N.Z.) Ltd, 182–190 Wairau Road, Auckland 10,
New Zealand

Penguin Books Ltd, Registered Offices: Harmondsworth,
Middlesex, England

First published by Dutton, an imprint of Dutton Signet,
a division of Penguin Books USA Inc.
Distributed in Canada by McClelland & Stewart Inc.

50 49 48 47 46

 REGISTERED TRADEMARK—MARCA REGISTRADA

Library of Congress Cataloging Card Number: 64–19538

Picture Credits

Jacket photograph, ROGER WOLTERS
End papers, JOAN SYDLOW
Dedication, R. A. WOLTERS

JOAN SYDLOW. All photographs, with the exception of
those listed below

BERNI SCHOENFIELD. Pages 86, 89, 94, 95, 96, 97,
126, 127, 142, 143, 156, 157, 158, 159,
160, 161, 164, 165, 166, 167

RICHARD A. WOLTERS. Page 78

ROGER WOLTERS. Pages 38, 44, 45, 46, 47, 48, 49,
50, 51, 52, 53, 54, 55, 66B, 67, 69L, 76L,
90, 94, 95, 118, 119, 120, 121, 136, 137,
144, 145

GENE HILL. Pages 146, 147

JOE VAN DENBURG. Pages 178, 179

Book and jacket design by R. A. WOLTERS
ISBN 0-525-24734-3

Printed in the United States of America

Dedicated to Retrievers and what they retrieve

Gene Hill's Tippy

Contents

Introduction

To one whose successful, lifelong resistance against the universal urge to write a book has been due in large part to respectful appreciation of the terrors and infinite miseries inherent in authorship, Richard A. Wolters must always be a phenomenon. Indeed, I think he may be that rarest of the species homo sapiens litterarius — a two-legged mammal whose four-chambered heart and reasoning intellect cannot comprehend fear.

I do not, of course, refer to organic fear; quite likely Wolters is as craven as the next of us in the presence of physical danger. But the misgivings which plague ordinary writers, fear of failure, of scorn, of moral challenge, of ridicule — these this odd-ball does not know exist.

Four years ago, Dick Wolters was an amiable trout fisherman who laid out a nice line, an inoffensive skeet shooter who occasionally scored a 25, a weekend camper and bird-hunter. He never had written so much as "I See the Cat."

But he had met a setter named Beau, turned him into a stylish hunter in one-third the time required by professional trainers, and concluded that he had stumbled upon a revolutionary training method which should belong to the world. He seized a typewriter and was off.

Since that day he has spawned three books, WATER DOG being the third. The first was GUN DOG, the story of Beau, and the second was FAMILY DOG, the saga of Tar, a sporting dog pet, and how he became a gentleman by the Wolters method of behavior tutelage. The first two were hugely successful as I predict this will be.

I was a bystander at the whelping of all three and I consider it no small tribute to the quality of my patience that I should be invited to write this introduction. To be qualified, I have shot pheasants, woodcock, and grouse over Beau's beautiful head, applauded Tar's drawing-room manners, and witnessed the field performances of Tar and Jock, the heroes of WATER DOG. Of course, I also had to read the books.

But I have enjoyed each step of the adventurous way with Dick and the dogs — and the books. Good luck, good hunting, and good sales to all of them.

ART SMITH
N.Y. Herald Tribune
Outdoor Editor

Author's Note

I sit in my camper, my traveling house on wheels, someplace in Connecticut. We're parked in a big field — that is, Jock, Tar, and I are parked here. Can't see much of the field now, it's almost dark. Jock and Tar are not interested in seeing anything now anyway. They're asleep on the rug at my feet.

A few hours ago this place was buzzing with people and dogs. It was a good day for our team as I look back. Excuse me a second as I take a sip from my new silver mug . . . Jock's first-place win in the Derby. Tar's turn in the field trials comes tomorrow.

As I look back, another reason the day was a success: between events I came back to Lablubber's Landlubber, the name of our camping coach, and typed the last words that go into this book. Jock's already won his prize. I won't know if I've won mine until you read it. But before you do, let me tell you about some fine folks who helped me.

Joan Sydlow you may have met before. She took the pictures in the first book GUN DOG. Her pictures in this book are just as fine, if that's possible. Joan, I raise Jock's cup and drink to you and your pictures.

Berni Schoenfield at this moment is sitting in Argentina drinking from his own cup. He's photographing duck hunting and trout fishing à la Argentina for some of our national magazines. Berni, Jock's cup to you, too, for the pictures in WATER DOG.

Son Roger took some of these pictures also. He took all the pictures in FAMILY DOG. Excuse me a moment, I have to refill Jock's cup.

Let's drink to Jock's mother. Well, that is his foster mother. Helen Ginnel's Whygin Kennel was his birthplace. It's also the birthplace of a lot of discussions that found their way, one way or another, into this book. Helen's home is also unofficial headquarters of the Westchester Retriever Club. We don't pay rent, but we should. To all the members, your triumphs and mistakes are also in the book. Jock's cup to them.

To Gene Hill, who has argued dog facts with me now on three books — Gene, let's breed your Tippy to my Jock. With their ability and what we know, that is, if we could teach them what we know with their ability, or I mean . . . oh, hell, Jock's cup to their wedding.

To wife Olive. A toast to our wedding and for allowing eight more dirty black feet into our home.

Jock, the last dram to you. It's been your day.

Tar, there is no more to drink, or I would have a sip to your tomorrow and tomorrows.   R. A. W.

Part I

Chapter 1

Why This Book?

Since I'm a guy who can't even find his shoes when he gets up in the morning, it's paradoxical that this book can teach you how to train your retriever to do his job. Maybe this isn't so odd after all. Many hours have been spent in bed figuring out the problems of shoe retrieving, and much has been learned. Remembering where the shoes were dropped eight hours before presents a challenging test. The object is to run the bedroom obstacle course for this complicated double retrieve in the shortest period of time to keep the feet from getting cold. Most difficult is when the retriever didn't see where the shoes landed the night before. Blind retrieves before coffee take patience and skill. So, if you can find your shoes in the morning you have demonstrated that you have what it takes to train a retrieving dog.

I have no figures on how many shoes are lost every year, but our Government has stated that for every five birds shot in the field one is lost because a trained retrieving dog was not used.

However, this is not a book on bedroom experience. It's *Water Dog*, a book for the waterfowl hunter and the field trialer. It's a how-to-train book. If you're an upland bird hunter and are interested in the pointing dogs, you have the wrong volume. We wrote that book, *Gun Dog*, a few years ago. We're not going to tell you here how to housebreak your puppy, comb him, de-flea him, feed him, medicate him, lift him or teach him parlor tricks. Anybody, even a six-year-old child, can do those things while making a dog into a good citizen. All this was shown in *Family Dog*. No, this is a retriever training book. I repeat the word *training* because we shall not take up valuable pages with field trial listings, standards or history of the breeds, field trial regulations or lists of clubs. For a five-cent stamp you can get all that free from the AKC.

What about choice of retrieving breed? You didn't ask me when you picked your wife. If you're satisfied with that choice, you ought to be able to pick out a dog. If you didn't do well in that choice, you should have learned something.

Books can tell you under what conditions which breed is best, and field trials prove them wrong. Most people say the black Labrador is best. That's because most own black Labs. They've won more field trials — of course, more have been entered. Yes, statistics show that the Lab comes out best, but don't underestimate the Goldens. They are a great dog. You can quote statistics until you're blue in the face to owners of Goldens or Chesapeake Bay retrievers, and they still wouldn't give you a plugged nickel for a black Lab, a yellow Lab, or even a pink spotted one.

Don't tell me that I'm hedging on this question of which breed. In the last trial I was in, my Lab was beaten so badly by a Golden that both dog and man went home with our tails between our legs. But, after that trial, I still wouldn't have traded my stupid, slow, thickheaded, black ignoramus for that fine, fast, smart Golden genius. Just luck, I guess, that I started with black Labradors.

To be sure that you'll feel the same way about your dog, if you haven't already decided on which breed, get out to a field trial. Watch the dogs work. The big three, in order, are the Lab, the Golden, and the Chessie. If you can find the flat coat, curly-coat retriever or the Irish water spaniel working, don't overlook them.

One serious consideration should be the dog's coat. Briars and burrs raise havoc with the Golden and the spaniels. So, if you live in an area with this kind of cover think again about the Lab, who, incidentally, does not have a doggy odor when wet.

If you're happy with the second-floor parlormaid and want to keep her contented, consider the poodle; they don't shed much. A group of sportsmen on the Eastern Shore are breeding and seriously using royal standard poodles as their duck dogs. Don't snicker. They're a lot smarter than some duck hunters I know.

It's always a good idea to take a look around in your area to see what breed the other hunters have settled on. You may want to breed later on. If you do it seriously it can be a lot of fun. But if you are only going to do it for fun my advice is to leave the breeding job to the professionals. They do it better, and you won't save any more even if you do do it right.

I assume you're able to make your own decision about the dog you're going to live with for the next fourteen or so years. And that's the last word I'll say on things that I won't tell you about. Except . . . Oh, yes, I forgot. I won't tell you how to build a kennel or how to show your dog in a beauty pageant.

Retrievers have been trained for hundreds of years, maybe even thousands. We're going to give you some new information about how a dog learns, and show you how to use it. We'll give you a new training tool for the job. And, very important in this busy world that we live in today, we'll show you how to do the job fast.

To whom is this book directed? Both the hunter and the field trialer. I'd like to think that the hunter takes precedence. Unlike the pointing dogs, retrievers are trained to do a parallel job in the hunting field and the trial field.

How much longer this will be true is a question that I can't answer. Field trials are supposed to be tests that simulate hunting conditions. But unfortunately fads develop in trials that gradually take the sport further and further away from hunting and make trialing a sport unto itself. This is especially true in the pointing breeds where speed, stamina and ground covered are the qualities most desired. The only way a man can keep up with such a dog is on horseback. Let me ask you: When was the last time you were invited to go bird shooting on horseback? No, a field trial pointer that works a woodcock patch halfway down the valley is useless in my book.

The thing that can spoil the trials for the retrievers is that there has been a tremendous surge in the popularity of the retriever breeds and the sport of field trialing. It's possible that soon there will be so many well-trained dogs that in order to find an out-and-out winner; field trial judges will be forced to make tests for the dogs that will contradict instead of complement hunting situations. Maybe the salvation will be more duck hunters so that participants and judges alike will keep real hunting conditions as the basis for trials.

Among the niceties of retrievers training is the fact that you can do it all year long. You don't have to have the duck season open to give your dog a good workout. You don't even need real live birds as you do with the pointing and flushing breeds. A dead duck can be used for months if you don't mind the smell; refrigeration between times helps. You don't need as much land (and it's getting precious these days) and you don't have to go to game farms which can cost a lot of undeductible green stuff. In fact, for the man who can only afford to be a one-dog man, the retrievers are the cheapest of all the hunting dogs to train. They're the most versatile, too. Although they are considered to be the waterfowler's dog, don't underestimate them as upland game-bird dogs.

Don't tell me about Joe's pointer Jack that will retrieve ducks. Put Jack in the kind of weather and water conditions that you work a retriever in, and you would kill him.

LAST THINGS FIRST

So often in the schooling of our youngsters you'll hear a kid say, "Why do I have to learn that?" It's really a good question and too often it goes unanswered. If there were only some way to explain and show children the final result of a subject, they might understand why they must learn the fundamental building blocks. How do you explain to a teenager why he must memorize a valence table for chemistry? You can only say to him that the valence table will be the language of the science and he won't understand why he must learn it until he learns it. So, being a responsible kid who can take direction, he goes to the telephone and talks to his girl for an hour.

But there are certain subjects that won't work that way. For the student who wants to be an architect, unless he's just goofing off, he can be shown "why" in language he can understand. The buildings around him are the living proof of why he has to sweat through solid geometry.

So, I'm going to start off by showing you the last chapter first. I'm going to show you the finished product; then I'll show you how to start from scratch to build it step by step. With the final product well in mind, you'll better understand the reasons for the fundamentals.

Communication is the key for getting any job done. First you'll have to learn the language; then you must teach it to your dog.

The great mistake that so many retriever owners make is that they do not recognize the difference between what the dog is born with and the finished retriever.

What we hope to do for both you and your dog is to take advantage of basic instincts, give them a vocabulary, and then we'll have these inborn instincts under our control. Let me give you a very simple example. You don't have to teach a retriever *how* to swim, but you will want to teach him *when* to swim.

How to swim is instinctive.

When to swim is a learned control.

The next step will be to develop the instincts and then implement the controls. From your language the dog must learn *where* to swim and *what* he's swimming for.

Where to swim is a highly developed control; your language will be voice, whistle and hand signals, plus a little language that would shock your mother.

What to swim for is important because you'd look rather stupid serving a decoy to your dinner guests.

My job of training you to train a retriever will be more like training a student to be an architect rather than a chemist. We can show you what the finished job looks like before you start.

I guess I'll never forget KO. For some reason a man always remembers the first.

She was a big retriever who lived right in the middle of the grouse country near Greene, New York. Now, the hunters up in that neck of the world don't give a tinker's damn for duck. The partridge is their bird. Bill Bartlett and Bob Maxon know every piece of bird cover. They study the habitats of the grouse all year and wouldn't tell their own grandmothers where the birds are in October. How KO, a retriever, got mixed up with this breed of man is really not known. Their dogs are setters; they had the best.

While we were drinking some "iced tea" in front of the fire after the first day's grouse hunt, KO, a misfit in this world, walked into the room, gave me a nasty look, shoved me out of the way and took my place at the fire. I gave way to her hundred-odd pounds, and since I was a guest in her home I decided I'd try to be polite. As I lifted my hand to pat her, she rolled her big brown eyes up to mine, outstared me, as much as to say, "Don't you dare touch me." Everybody just watched silently.

Out of embarrassment I turned to Bill and said sheepishly, "Fine-looking dog." And then, to change the subject, I stupidly said, "I've never shot duck over a retriever."

That did it. Some old decoys were found and all was arranged for dawn the next morning. Bill said we'd take KO. She had never been field trained but was a fine hunting dog.

'Til my dying day I'll be leery of the man and the dog when I hear that phrase — "never been field trained but a fine hunting dog."

Before dawn, half-frozen in my light bird-hunting clothes, I was crouched on the edge of a swamp pond. Five of us and KO had the joint surrounded. A flight of wood duck came in. I saw them swing my way. My heart pounded — not because it looked like I was going to get a shot, but the wood duck is the most treasured of all ducks for the trout fisherman who ties his own flies. And that's me. The skin of a wood duck, if you can find one, goes for at least ten bucks.

As the drake set his wings, I led the bird, shot, and in my usual style had to shoot the other barrel to drop him. A two years' supply of dry-fly wings bobbed on the water! In my excitement I forgot to reload my gun. This point should be remembered for the rest of this story.

Trying to be nonchalant about my prize, I called across the pond and asked Bill to send KO to make the retrieve. But KO, hearing the shots, had broken and was already well on her way. But this "hunting dog" swam right for a decoy. I threw a stick at the drifting bird which, thank goodness, was within my throwing distance. KO saw the splash, swam over, picked up the bird.

I coaxed her toward me with every good name in the book. I was just about ready to forgive her for what she had done to me the night before when she walked out on an island twenty feet offshore and proceeded to eat my $10.00. Twelve dozen trout flies were being consumed by that monster. I yelled, jumped, stamped, screamed, and cursed. She munched.

I bit my lip and proceeded to make a blundering mistake. I picked up a stout stick and heaved it at her. She casually dropped the bird. She took a few steps toward me and my unloaded gun. She rolled those big brown eyes up to meet mine as much as to say, "For a guy with an unloaded gun you're pretty tough. Do that again, Buster, and you'll be dessert." She went back and finished the duck, leaving me 20 cents' worth of feathers which I couldn't reach.

Many years later I ran into Bill and asked him how KO was. "Well . . ." he said slowly, "every dog's allowed one bite. KO bit every member of the family once and then it was my turn; that's when I got rid of her!"

HERE'S HOW THE JOB SHOULD BE DONE
HERE'S YOUR VOCABULARY

A working retriever generally walks at *heel*. This is not only convenient and keeps him out of the way of the gun, but in most duckhunting situations he'll do all his work from this place next to you.

A *non-slip retriever* will not slip: just what it says. He won't leave your side until commanded to do so. This is not just to demonstrate control and the niceties of life. It can be shown very simply that a dog who *breaks*, prematurely *bolts*, or runs out to retrieve a bird on hearing the shot will not be able to *mark* the fall. *Unsteady* young dogs will invariably rush toward the fall, hunt short, and then after a while will forget where the bird fell, leave the *area of fall* and start wandering all over the lot.

He'll eventually come up with the bird if his mother and father endowed him with a good basic hunting drive. But his parents can't help him if your parents endowed you with a good shooting eye and while he broke and ran for one bird you dropped another behind you in the swamp.

A hunting dog must sit and watch all the action and go into action only when told. As an adult he should be required to mark and remember *single, double* or *triple* falls, their direction and approximate distance.

To make these *marked* retrieves, falls that he has seen, the dog should not *pop*; that is, he should not stop and look back to the handler for directions or help.

If you have crippled a bird over land, your dog will be expected to use his nose to track and run the cripple down. It has always been a joke in my family that I got my nose from my Uncle Lewie; it never looked good or worked well. Retrievers inherit good noses, but you'll have to teach them to use it by taking advantage of the wind. He'll also have to use his nose in the situation of a *bad fall* where the bird was downed in extremely heavy cover.

Retrievers are rugged, hard-going dogs. They have a strong hunting desire and can be worked as a flushing dog much like the spaniel. For the hunter, the retriever is an all-around dog. He'll quarter a field, flush the game, be steady for shot, and then retrieve. When that job's done he can put on his other hat when you put on your quilted duck clothes. While you shiver, he'll quiver with anticipation, awaiting the first plunge into an icy pond for a mallard.

In some areas where the pointing dog is king and it's thought that the retrieving job might interfere with his highness' pointing ability, retrievers are kept at heel, then sent in after the action is over to bring home the game. Well, whatever his job, the retriever is a willing, anxious, happy worker . . . he'll baby-sit for you, too.

Let's re-examine that phrase — "a good hunting dog, but not trained." All that means is that the dog is hunting by its instincts. He's taking no directions from you, can ruin some good shooting, can cost you lost birds, and maybe a friendship — especially if your companion has a well-trained dog along.

You and a duckhunting acquaintance are out for the first time together. Before sunup your rig is out and your dogs are settled. That is, his dog is watching the sky and yours wants to romp. There's something indecent about screaming at a dog before sunup, but that's only one strike against your team. When the first flight comes in from your side you drop a bird. Hunter, your dog, and the duck hit the water at the same instant. As he's swimming back with your trophy, you turn to your companion and wait for a statement of approval from him. He says something about a nice job. As Hunter hits the beach he drops the bird to shake, and turns to see if there are any other man-sized jobs for him to do. His *delivery* isn't the best, you say, but at least the duck is out of the water. Chuckle, chuckle. No use trying to have him bring it to hand. So you get up, step out of the blind to retrieve both dog and duck. Then, *damn* . . . you flare three black ducks swinging into the stool from your partner's side. Strike two.

After coffee, things seem a little friendlier in the blind. Old Headstrong wants action, so here it comes. Three broadbills, one's dumped. You could have really taken one too but you grabbed for Hunter; it's the other dog's turn. Knothead wouldn't know what the word *honor* means. So you hold him by the scruff of the neck while the retrieving job is being professionally handled. Strike three . . . Old Hardmouth bounds out of your grip, out of the blind, and wants to take the duck away from the other dog as he's finishing his retrieve up the beach. Result . . . a tug of war, a headless broadbill and a damn good dogfight. Make a mental note. The next time you make a date with your new friend — better it should be for golf.

Well, maybe all these things couldn't have happened on one duck hunt, but then again maybe no ducks would have flown and your acquaintance might still think old Hunter could be a pretty good dog from the stories you told while whiling away some bluebird weather in the blind.

On the other hand, just no use telling you what might have happened if one of those ducks was wing-shot and sailed down out of sight behind the island 200 yards out. From where Hunter was sitting he couldn't have seen the bird go down even if he was looking. A *blind* retrieve such as that would be impossible for him. He wouldn't know how to *take a line*; that is, go in the direction you send him, go straight and keep going until he hears a single whistle blast from you. Then he should turn, look at you to get his next instructions. If he's on the island at this time, he must sit and pay attention to you. If he's swimming he must dog paddle and watch for your hand signal: to the right, to the left, or *back*, that is, away from you. Or he must be able to come toward you on the "come-in" whistle command. The duck may be drifting on a strong tide, and it may be necessary to make a change of plan to make the retrieve. A swimming dog can't see very far ahead, so you have to be his navigator. You'll have to *handle* or direct him by hand signal and whistle.

The thing that so many duck hunters seem to forget when they talk about old Knuckle Head is that many, many of the hunting situations that they encounter do require handling of the dog.

The dog should be trained to do his job as fast as possible. He should be taught not to *switch* birds; that is, to retrieve one and then on his way in drop it to pick up another. True, he could be sent back to get the one he left, but extra time and confusion among the decoys aren't conducive for ducks to *stool*, among the decoys. Besides, you want your dog to learn to do a fast job to get him out of cold water as soon as possible.

While referring to dog safety, there are certain types of duckhunting where heavy decoy anchors and long lines are necessary. They can be very dangerous for the dog. A few years ago, while hunting in Long Island Sound, I witnessed what was almost such a tragedy. Eight guns and four dogs were taken by dory out to the shooting rocks. Decoys were set out from the boat, and parties of two hunters and one dog were dropped off. The dory would return for pickup in four hours. Unfortunately, I drew a "hasn't been trained but a good hunter" dog. On the first pass we dropped a duck behind the decoys. This "hunter" broke and made a beeline for the downed bird. I looked away as I saw him swim through the decoys, hoping what I thought was going to happen wouldn't happen. Looking back, I saw the blocks start to move. "Call him back," I shouted to the owner. But the dog was a "hunter"; he couldn't be handled. He drove on toward the drifting duck. More decoys started to move. The dog swam harder and moved slower. Realizing his plight he tried to untangle himself but only made matters worse. Frantically the dog started swimming in circles. More frantically the owner tried to whistle him in. No man could stand that January water, and no struggling dog was going to stand it long. I walked away. I never knew a whistle could say so much. Faster and faster, shriller and shriller it blew. Then it stopped. It was all over. I walked back from behind the rocks. My partner was up to the top of his waders in water. His head was extended forward, peering through the early fog. The whistle, now silent, was held two inches from his mouth. When he saw me he didn't speak . . . he pointed to sea. I looked, straining my eyes through the soup. Two hundred yards out, standing on top of the water like Jonah delivered back from the sea, stood the dog on an emerging rock. I nodded to my partner. He shouted over a wind that came up, "I prayed!"

God's ebbing tide answered.

As we sat to break out the coffee he asked, "How do you go about training a dog to handle?"

"Easy," I answered, then gulped some hot coffee.

Chapter 2

You Should Know That...

Gene Smith has a very special black Lab named Ruff. The two of them are hard workers for Ducks Unlimited. One of this team is the project chairman for the local DU chapter. He'll run dinners, trap and skeet shoots and any other boondoggle inside the law to raise money for unmarried ducks. But as a team their very special chore is to act something like a "welcome wagon." When a new family moves into a home that has at least four baths and the local ladies are knocking on the front door, Gene calls the new landowner on the phone and invites him for a day's duckhunting. He's been very successful getting donations for DU.

No one has ever understood why Gene has been so successful. After the day's hunt the guest never seems to want to talk about it, but Ducks Unlimited always receives a big donation at their next function. This has gone on for years . . . until a nonhunting city type moved into a four-and-a-half-bathroom house. Here's the story he told after the third drink the night he was invited to the country club to meet the members.

"I got an invitation from this nice chap to go duckhunting. I'd never shot, so I figured I'd give it a whirl. Before dawn I met him at his boat. He had a big black dog. We went out on the Sound in what he called a rig and set out what he called a stool and we turned the rig into what he called a blind. After we drank what he called coffee he suddenly shouted 'Mark'! Eyes heavenward, he knelt like a monk at the altar. The dog did the same. I thought they'd both flipped their lids. Their hypnotic eyes peered through the drifting fog. They seemed to be in a trance. Suddenly two ducks materialized from nowhere out of the eerie mist. Bang! Bang! They were dead.

"He turned to me still with a fanatical gaze and said, 'Watch this.'

"He said 'Back' to the dog, but the dog leaped forward . . .

"Out of the boat. He ran across the top of the water, picked up the duck, ran back to the boat and delivered the bird. A strange hand sign sent the dog off again scampering over the top of the water. In a moment he pranced back with the second bird."

This chap then relaxed and asked me what I thought of that. I had to be honest, and told him the truth.

"That damn dog can't even swim."

TWO WAYS TO USE RETRIEVERS

This story, which Gene can tell even better than I do, has softened up many a guy for a donation at the Connecticut Ducks Unlimited Dinner. If the story were true, Ruff would have an important purpose in life. Unfortunately, Ruff really can swim, but he still has a job. Gene uses him as a gun dog, and I swear that Ruff can distinguish between a Black and a Merganser in flight.

It would be a shame to use such a fine dog only as a house pet or in the show ring. A good retriever should work. They'll be happier and so will you. But there are two ways to use them as working dogs. One is as a gun dog and the other is for field trials.

Unfortunately, for many people field trials are becoming the end product and not the means to the end. Many highly trained retrievers have never seen a real duck blind, and their owners think a double barrel is an extra-large quantity of beer.

I feel sure the reader has already received an idea of what he should expect of a gun dog. For the novice trainer and trial-handler, we should look at field trials to show them what they're getting themselves into.

At one time, and not so very long ago, it was only the wealthiest families with professionally trained and handled dogs who were active in the sport of field trials. But the sociology of our country is changing. Almost every area has its field trial club, their members from all walks of life.

The man who is going to buy a pup, raise and train him, should realize he has about as much chance of having a great field trial champion as the man who has a half a buck in his jeans, puts it into a one-arm bandit and expects to win the jackpot.

This is not to say that it can't be done. But it will take a tremendous amount of work and time to produce a machine that will consistently score on the trial circuit. The man who has the time, the training area, the know-how, can produce a dog as fine as a professional's dog. For many, the sport of the field trials is to lick the professional. It's tough, but can be done.

Breeding alone is not the answer to a great dog. If it were, the game would be simple. Pups from champion stock don't necessarily become champions. There have been some national champions who never threw a great dog. On the other hand, one dog was bought for fifty dollars from some obscure litter, nursed through distemper to go on to win the National Championship twice.

The answer is a combination of many things: breeding, training, ability, time and money.

Take a look at your checkbook. Whatever that balance, it'll have nothing to do with the amount of pleasure you're going to get from your retriever. But it can determine what you can achieve on the licensed field trial circuit, barring the luck of the sweepstake winner. Campaigning a dog through the trial circuit takes a fat bundle in entrance fees alone, without figuring the cost of the traveling.

So, what about field trials? If you like golf, it would be a mistake not to play because you could never be National Open Champion. If you can develop a good game, you'll get a lot of fun out of the local competition. And this should be a satisfying goal with your dog. Develop a good game whether it be field trials and/or duckhunting.

The point of this discussion is not to discourage anyone from getting interested in field trials. Quite the contrary, field trialing is a lot of fun. If there's a local field trial club, seek it out and join. The club will give the dog the opportunity to get plenty of work all year long, not just during the open hunting season. You'll meet some wonderful people. It's always a satisfying pleasure to be with other people who have a common interest. Even more important, you'll learn a lot, fast, about handling and training your dog. Dog people are even worse know-it-alls than Aunt Sadie's Tuesday bridge club . . . everyone has his own theories which he'll express at the shuffle of the cards or the drop of a leash.

TIME BECOMES A FACTOR

There are two distinct ways to train the upland pointing dogs, for hunting or for field trials. Unlike the pointing dog, the retriever's job is fairly similar in a duck blind or in a field trial, but we're still going to train them differently. Remember, this book is basically for the duck hunter. That means that the training will be the same as if we were going to field trial the dog, but we're going to take the dog at a faster pace than field trials demand. The man who owns one dog and has him as a house pet and also as his duck-hunting companion doesn't have to and shouldn't wait until the dog is past two years old before he starts to train him to do the complete job in the field.

Let's expand this very important point.

First, grant the fact that the Seeing-Eye dog gets the most rigorous training a dog can receive. If this dog can be started in his advance training at the age of one year, and ninety days later is a finished companion, the eyes, for his blind master, why in the name of common sense can't your retriever be started in his advanced work before he is two years old? There is no difference in the dogs. Many of the Seeing-Eye dogs are Labradors and Goldens.

Starting the retriever in his advanced work even before he's a year old will startle many a field trialer, but if they will face the facts honestly and squarely they'll see that it can be done successfully.

The traditional demands of the field trials do not take into consideration that much has been learned in the past few years about the mental development of the dog. As you read on, you'll see that the scientists have proved that the dog's learning ability develops much faster than we ever expected.

But man is a creature of habit. Once the pattern is set, it takes much time and work for him to change his ways.

The pattern of field trial tests has been established for many years. It calls for a dog to be considered a Derby dog until his second birthday. Most trainers will not allow their dogs to be taught advanced lessons until he's two because they honestly believe that the too rapid advancement will hinder the dog's marking ability and his progress. This book is not to try to prove them wrong. This book is not to convince them to change their ways. That is why I address the book to the hunter; he will not be hindered in his training by the specific tests set up for the field trial. He'll want his dog to advance step by step according to the amount of time he can put into the training. He can have a competent working dog in his duck blind when the dog is one year old.

I've heard experienced field trialers snicker at such a statement, but I've seen their eyes pop when a nine-months-old puppy was handled to a 100-yard blind retrieve in water to bring back a seven-pound goose.

As an example, the first step in handling a retriever is to have him stop, turn and sit facing you on one whistle blast. This isn't ordinarily taught to a Derby dog. He learns to do this only after he's two. Teaching him to do this at two years of age can take some rough going for the dog and trainer. But there's no reason why a Derby dog can't learn to sit on whistle before he learns to sit by voice command. There's no reason why a dog can't be stopped by whistle at any distance within hearing range by the time he's four or five months old, let alone until after two years. We'll show you later how to do it even sooner.

For those of you who are wondering just what the requirements are for a field trial Derby dog, let me spell them out for you.

The dog is brought to *line*, the starting place. He is commanded to sit at your side by blowing one blast on the whistle. The judge stands behind the dog and handler. When all are ready, the judge signals for the birdboy to release the bird for the guns to shoot. The test will consist of a single or a double retrieve. After the bird or birds are down, the judge tells you to send the dog. The dog must not break. He may go only on command; then he is on his own. These are marking and remembering tests. They are good hunting tests and sometimes very difficult. But these dogs are capable of more advanced education at this age. In fact, the commands for advanced training are more easily taught to the dog when he is young!

In spite of the fact that I declare that this book is not intended for the field trialer, this accelerated training method can be a tremendous advantage to the training of field trial dogs.

First decide if you are going to train for the field or for trials. If you're going to trial the dog, advance him according to his ability. If started properly, any six-month-old retriever can be taught to handle. We will show you step by step how to do it. But here is the essence: Teach him to handle under yard training conditions only. A fifty-foot yard is big enough. Teach him to stop on whistle at any given spot in the yard. Teach him to follow your hand direction signals in this controlled area. As a very young pup he will learn to the right, to the left and back in a matter of a week or so. Within a few weeks of this you can hide a dummy in the yard and he'll even learn to do these simple blind retrieves. But there is something even more important that he is learning at this tender age. If he follows your hand signals and finds a dummy, he'll learn to believe in you. This is the most important factor in training a retriever. Let me repeat this: If a dog learns that if you give him a signal and he follows it he'll get a reward — the dummy — he'll not just be learning the signal itself; but, more important, he'll be learning *to believe in you*, the teacher.

Now he has learned the simple rudiments of the advanced handling commands. If the dog is going to be field trialed and you're afraid that the hand signals will cause him to pop and depend on you for directions, never give these handling commands in the field. Keep this as a training game always in the same yard location. If you never handle him outside of this controlled area, he'll never come to expect to be handled in the field. But when you're ready to teach handling in the field at age two, he'll already know the commands, and the transfer will be ready for both of you.

Let's step back a moment and take a broad look at all hunting dogs. See if this won't convince you that the longer you delay with a retriever, the more difficult your job is going to be. First, I should like to show you why the retriever must learn to believe in you. Later I'll call on more scientific findings to show you why the training must take place at an early age.

The rabbit hound believes in his nose and the chase.

The pointing dog believes in his nose and the gun.

The retriever believes in his handler.

Here's the explanation:

The rabbit hunter's dog is a self-hunter. You put him on the trail of a rabbit and he either goes off a-howling or you get rid of him. If he won't hunt of his own accord, you can't teach him to do it — just something about his genes: either he will or he won't. If he does go off for Brer Rabbit he goes after him for himself. He wants that rabbit. He's not hunting for the gun. It just so happens that the rabbit runs in big circles within the area of his hole. If the dog stays on the trail long enough, and the hunter stays put he'll eventually have a shot.

The bird hunter's dog hunts for the gun. You can never teach a bird dog *to* hunt; you can only teach him *how* to hunt. He quarters the field seeking out the game. When he finds it he stops dead in his tracks, and his rigid position points to the fact that game is near. The hunter moves in for the flush and the kill. This dog can be trained to work in close to you for woodcock hunting or at a great distance in open country for quail. A good bird dog will stay on point 'til hell freezes over or until the hunter finds him and makes the bird flush. Old-time pointer trainers all tell a variation of the story about old Blue, the dog that was lost for a month. Finally, one day while hunting they found his skeleton on point.

The duck hunter finds his own game. His dog never goes into action until the game is down. He's trained to sit at heel during all the action. His job is then to retrieve the downed game either on water or land. He does his job directly for you, not your gun. The bird dog is on his own; the retriever is on his own after a certain point; then he works directly, dependent on the handler. Often in upland bird hunting a pointing dog is given a whistle and hand signal to move on, and the dog just won't go. A good hunter won't insist that the dog obey; instead the hunter will go to the dog and let him hunt out the area. The hunter soon learns that a good bird dog knows more about where the birds are than the hunter does. But this just isn't so with the retriever. In most cases if man pays attention he can mark a downed bird better than the dog. As we have discussed before, often in a hunting situation the dog never sees where the bird fell, or tide waters or wind will drift a duck. A trained retriever will go any place, under any conditions, for you.

He'll do it on his own if he knows where the game has fallen or he'll faithfully follow your directions, knowing that you'll lead him to the bird. A dog who works this close with you has to believe in you.

You can never teach a rabbit hound *to* hunt or *how* to hunt.

You can never teach a bird dog *to* hunt only *how* to hunt.

You can teach a retriever *both*.

This dog is going to learn your every desire. He'll learn to work from heel and retrieve on command whether it be land or water. He'll learn to follow your whistle and hand signals. He'll learn when to do the retrieving job on his own and when to depend on you. I think the bond between dog and man is stronger in the retriever breeds than in any of the other hunting dogs because of the basic requirement of the teamwork necessary to get the job done.

Our real goal is this teamwork; field trial stylishness and success is one by-product. The upland bird work your retriever does will be another by-product.

Chapter 3

The Dog's Mental Development

(A New Training Method)

Did you ever go to a cocktail party that turned out to be a bloody bore? Next time you're forced to bend elbows, elbow to elbow, go armed with a few choice statements about the local school system. Any stupid statement will do. Example: "Kids learn best with a nasty teacher." When the party has reached the pinnacle of boredom, release your statements in a firm voice. Then sidle away to the bar. Take your drinks to a neutral corner, pull up a stool and watch Round One begin.

Of course, everybody is an expert on education. They've all been to school. I've seen them battle to the death, defending the way they were taught.

A word of warning: make sure there's no professional educator on board who really knows what he's talking about . . . they're positively anesthetic.

I'm an old hand at this game, an experienced provocateur. I have been doing this needling for years.

Now I'm looking for a new hobby. I went to a post-field-trial cocktail party, and injected my usual needling remark at the appropriate moment: "A dog should be started in his training when he's weaned." I forgot to get my drink. I tried to get to a neutral corner. There wasn't any.

Next morning my wife sat smugly across the breakfast table and politely said, "Your fine needle was sure smashed with a sledgehammer last night . . . dear."

Conclusion: Never mess with a cocktail party of dog people. If you're going to make a statement about dog-training theory, quote someone else. That's what I'm about to do now.

When I began to train dogs I employed the by-gosh and by-gum method. The idea of starting a puppy very, very early in his training seemed right, by-gosh, so by-gum I tried it. It worked! It just seemed logical that any animal that was going to be trained should receive the training as soon as it was ready and willing to accept it. It naturally follows that this prevents the learning of bad habits and, even more important, eliminates the difficult process of unlearning.

I was just about convinced that early training was the answer to dog training, which I am sure was not a unique thought, when I heard about the work of Dr. J. Paul Scott, social psychologist, Rhodes scholar, and director of the Animal Behavior Laboratory at Hamilton Station. A visit to Hamilton Station, which is part of the Roscoe B. Jackson Memorial Laboratory, Mount Desert Island, Maine, was an exciting experience.

After my trip to Maine I couldn't wait 'til the next field trial cocktail party. For weeks I worked over the details and prepared my statement. It would go something like this: "The business we all learned in school about a one-year-old dog being like a seven-year-old boy; a two-year-old dog being like a fourteen-year-old boy; a three-year-old dog being like a twenty-one-year-old man; and a seven-year-old dog being like a man about ready to go over the hill is bunk!" If that doesn't raise enough fuss, "A dog should be started in his training at age 49 days."

I'd sneak to the bar for a drink, but instead of taking a ringside seat I'd come back to fight this one out. What a fine new hobby! I could picture my wife across the breakfast table smiling and saying, "Last night you were magnificent . . . dear."

I can hear myself now, spouting Dr. J. Paul Scott's theories as if they were my own.

I can hear my profound opening statement: "When to start training a puppy and how he learns go hand in hand. The correct time to start a pup will depend on his mental development."

That should capture the audience. Now it's just a matter of courage . . .

* * * * * * *

Unfortunately, starting a pup in the past was based on his physical development, not his mental ability. Hence the old wives' tale of the seven-to-one ratio, the dog of one year being compared to a boy of seven years, etc. Scientists have shown that this seven-to-one ratio is only a *physical* comparison between man and dog, and has nothing to do with the *mental* development of dogs. What I've seen would make a mental ratio more like eighteen-to-one. A one-year-old dog can perform on his level of work as an eighteen-year-old boy can on his level.

But in order to get the year-old dog performing at his maximum potential, the desire to learn and the correct learning attitude must be instilled in the dog. Therefore, it's only logical that the dog should come to you with no problems, and the trainer should have control over his development from the beginning. Sensitive or bullheaded dogs are not born; they're made. Eager workers are also made. Luck is not a factor of training. Neither the professional nor the amateur trainer has time to waste. So often in the past the professional thought he was saving time by waiting until a pup was six months or a year old before he started to train the dog. He was waiting to see what potential the dog would show naturally. This may have saved time, but much talent was wasted. The amateur trainer should never wait. He'll most likely have only one dog and will fall in love with it, and if he waits months before starting training he'll end up with a dud.

This new scientific finding leaves no doubt about it: *A puppy should be taken home and started in his training at the exact age of 49 days.*

If a puppy lives in a kennel too long with no human contact and training, you're adding a great big unknown factor to your training problem when you take him home. Many kennels are recognizing this and are giving the puppies of a litter "training and play" periods. This helps to a degree, but it is not enough. Your pup should be taken away from his litter mates on the 49th day. During this seven-week period the dog got a sense of competition in the litter, but the social order — or what the scientists call the pecking order — hasn't as yet had time to form his personality. Staying with the litter can be almost as damaging to his future ability as a learner as the lack of human contact can be. All litters develop this pecking order. Here is where the headstrong bully and the wallflower personalities develop. Either one can be a hindrance in training.

Let's take a look at the work Dr. Scott and his team of researchers performed at Hamilton Station. This work was done in conjunction with Guide Dogs for the Blind, Inc.

Seeing-Eye dogs receive the most rigorous and exacting training of any dogs. For years it was believed that breeding was the answer to supplying puppies for this training. The breeding of the very finest Seeing-Eye dogs produced litters from which only 20 percent of the puppies had the ability, it seemed, to go through the rigid training to become Guide Dogs. In recent years the demand for these trained dogs has been greater than the supply. Dr. Scott and his team of workers sought and found the answer to the supply problem. It was a new approach to training. That new training method is *acceleration*.

Scientific study showed that there are five critical periods of a pup's life, five phases of his mental development. The shocking thing is that they all take place before the dog is sixteen weeks old. By this time the dog's brain has reached its adult form and size but, of course, without adult experience. So, instead of waiting for the puppy to grow up so it could be trained, Dr. Scott's work proved that it was actually harmful to delay. Starting the training early under the new accelerated program, the experimenters produced *90 percent success* in litters of the same breeding that produced only 20 percent under the traditional methods of training. Many observers first thought that this outstanding success might be because of the exacting conditions of the scientific training procedures. When the accelerated training method was put into actual practice in Seeing-Eye kennels and training programs, one full year's program even outstripped the laboratory results — 94 percent of all litters successfully completed the rigorous training. This certainly is proof that early training can produce hitherto unbelievable results.

FIRST CRITICAL PERIOD — 0 TO 21 DAYS

Zero to 21 days is the first critical period. During these three weeks the pup's mental capacity is almost zero. The pup reacts only to his needs — warmth, food, sleep, and its mother. If anything at all could be taught, it would be strictly in the area of survival, such as a simple test of getting food. Abruptly on the 21st day his senses seem to function. He's like a house that's been built and wired for all the electrical appliances but has not been hooked up to the current. Then on the specific day the juice is applied and every-thing starts to function. In all breeds of dogs this happens on the 21st day of life. This leads immediately to the second critical period.

SECOND CRITICAL PERIOD — 21 TO 28 DAYS

The 21st to the 28th day is the time of the second phase — it's when the pup absolutely needs Momma. During this week the dog's senses function, the brain and nervous system start to develop, and the big new world around him can be a pretty frightening experience. The emotional and social stress of life will have the greatest impact on him during this week. Removal from mother at this time could be catastrophic.

THIRD CRITICAL PERIOD — 28 TO 49 DAYS

From 28 to 49 days is the third period of development. Slowly the dog reacts to his surroundings. He ventures away from Mother to explore the world around him. It's at the end of this period that the dog's nervous system and his brain will have developed to the capacity of an adult but, of course, without the experience. He'll be ready to recognize people and respond to the voice. He'll have spent enough time in the litter to know that he's a dog. This may sound strange, but it has been shown that puppies taken from the litter too soon were difficult to breed later on. They just never got the idea that they were dogs. It's also during this third period that the social order or pecking order of the litter starts to form. This means the pups that learn to get in and fight for their food will tend to become bullies and the pups that are cowed by the more aggressive pups will become shy and develop wall-flower personalities. It's desirable for the pup to live in the litter long enough for him to get a little competitive spirit from his family life, but too much is harmful. The puppy is now ready to learn, and learn he will; so it's better for you to get into the picture at this point and have him learn the things that will mold the type of personality that you want the dog to have.

Up until this time the dog was too young to take from the mother, and does benefit from the social situation of the litter. But when *the dog is ex-actly 49 days old*, although he will be physically immature, his brain will have attained its full adult form.

FOURTH CRITICAL PERIOD — 49 TO 84 DAYS

The trainer and the dog should start to get to know each other *now*, not a week later or a week earlier. Dr. Scott's research has shown that this, the

49th day, is the best time in a dog's life to establish the dog-human relationship. The person who's going to train the dog will, in effect, now take the place of the pup's mother. Through feeding, playing, and general care of the dog at this age — seven to twelve weeks — a bond will be established that will have a permanent effect on the dog. At no later time in the dog's life will the pup have the ability to achieve as strong a bond or rapport with humans as at this age.

The research at the Behavior Laboratory showed that human contact in this seven- to twelve-week period is almost the whole key to the dog's future prospects. Puppies that were completely isolated for as little as the first sixteen weeks of life grew into dogs that were incapable of being trained, let alone becoming companion dogs.

Simple commands can be taught at this time. The teaching is at this point in the form of games. There should be no discipline, and by the time the dog is twelve weeks old — the end of the preschool or fourth critical stage of his development — the dog will know what is meant by commands SIT, STAY, COME, and possibly HEEL.

Getting settled in the new home is a very important part of his education. A secure puppy will be a happy dog and will take to learning and discipline.

The new information has shown that dogs can get what is called kennel blindness. They just eat and sleep and exist, waiting for someone to come and plunk down some money in order to take them home. Dogs that have had absolutely no human contact before sixteen weeks of age have little chance of becoming what we want in a companion. Dogs that have missed human contact for even thirteen weeks, and who were bred to become working dogs, may be completely untrainable as workers.

One of the most interesting aspects of the Seeing-Eye research was the information about interrupted training. Dogs started at a very early age, handled and trained through this fourth critical period — age twelve weeks — were then put back in the kennel situation. The lessons stopped for a period of only two weeks. After the two weeks, human contact and lessons were begun again, but only 57 percent of these dogs were able to go on to become Guide Dogs. When the formal lessons and human contact were stopped for three weeks, only 30 percent went on through the rigorous training to become guides. These facts dramatically show that to make the most of a dog, the training has to begin early and without interruption and be carried into the last critical phase of the puppy's development.

FIFTH CRITICAL PERIOD — 84 TO 112 DAYS

This fifth period — from 12 to 16 weeks — is when the puppy starts to school. The play-teaching games stop and the formal lessons start. The dog is ready to learn *disciplined* behavior. This is the time a young dog will declare his independence. At this time, dog and trainer resolve the problem of who's going to be boss. Deciding who's boss can be settled if the dog is started late, but it might take a two-by-four to do it.

We prepare the dog for learning in the seven- to twelve-week period. Fundamental training then begins at twelve weeks, and by the end of sixteen weeks this dog will know his basic commands and respond well to them.

This information is the same for all breeds, pure bred or not. What we're going to do is relate this material to the training of the retrieving dogs. I've heard handlers say that they started their dog at a year and have had fine results. What they don't know is how much better their dog could have been if the bond between teacher and student was made early. A child or dog that has a good early experience learning will enjoy learning, and they will learn to learn.

If this early training sounds a little startling to you, it's not just new in dog training. In Warren, Pennsylvania, and Brookline, Massachusetts, they are starting their children to school at age three years eight months. Educators say that these kids will have higher levels of social and emotional development and be happier and more self-sufficient human beings. Kids who have gone through this program continue to improve academically throughout their school years. These "early admits" also took part in significantly more extracurricular activities.

How far educators will carry this I don't know, but just last week I read an article in a national magazine on teaching children age two to read! I don't think to this day that the world recognizes the full impact of the first Russian Sputnik. We're now re-examining our old educational ideas.

HOW A DOG LEARNS

Most dogs don't learn anything useful to the owner because no one sees to it that they do; 95 percent of the almost 30 million dogs in this country are flea bags and affectionate parasites. They wag their tails; that pleases the master, so they get free room and board, medicare, unemployment compensation, and eventually social security plus your easy chair.

If you want a happy retriever, make him a worker; that's what he was bred for. I once went so far as to say that a good working dog would rather work than eat. I almost ended eating those words, but just before they were shoved down my throat I suggested an experiment. The dog was placed at heel, food was put down, and at the same time a bird was shot for the dog. He retrieved, delivered the bird, then ate his food. Then I had supper, and it sure tasted better than my words.

The ancient adage, "You can't teach an old dog new tricks," was written by some old dog who was just trying to get out of work. True, an old dog that has learned nothing can learn nothing, but a dog that has learned to learn will continue to learn all his life.

Both kids and dogs start out with a strong desire to please. As a parent, I sometimes wonder what happens to that desire. As a dog trainer, I find that a dog wants to please, all through his life. Some forward-thinking caveman threw some starving mutt a fat stewing bone — and for millions of years since, man has a grateful friend who wants to serve by pleasing. This becomes one of the most valuable training tools we have.

A dog responds to his master's display of pleasure or displeasure. There's always tension in a learning situation. Reward reduces the tension and gives pleasure. Reprimand or punishment increases the tension and produces discomfort. The dog's instinctive desire to please leads him to seek your pleasure. He tries to do what you want in order to receive your good graces. This we call learning.

The stronger you can build the urge to please in the puppy, the easier the training job is going to be on both of you. When the puppy is started in his training at seven weeks, just the fact that we care for and love him at that early age intensifies the rapport between teacher and pupil. At first there is no reprimand in the training — training is in the form of fun games. This helps to build the desire to please. As he develops, common sense on your part will show the way to balance reward and punishment properly to keep the learning mechanism going.

A dog learns by association. The learning process is a matter of repetition, more repetition, and still more, until it becomes a part of the dog's behavior. We then call it memory.

Dogs can be taught on two levels of learning — the conscious and the unconscious level — according to what is being taught.

Learning on the unconscious level is the learning that the dog does without being aware that he's learning. The dog is repeatedly put into a situation; the situation is duplicated so many times that the dog comes to react in a predictable manner. There is no reprimand or reward; the dog just does what he's expected to do because he has never done it any other way.

A good example of this is traveling and living in a dog crate in your car. At first he'll bark and raise hell, but he learns that the fuss gets him nowhere. He soon learns to love it. Another example is preparing the dog for the gun to prevent gunshyness. He just learns that a loud noise means something good instead of something to fear.

Learning on the conscious level is when the dog knows damn right well that he's being taught something. This learning is done in the formal lessons, and starts when the dog is twelve weeks old. The dog goes to school. Here is where common sense, love, affection, firmness, more firmness, and spankings are the teacher's devices.

You show the dog what you want. Example: command SIT. He finds out what your language means by trial and error. Once he has the idea, you put him through the action, give the command. He soon associates the action with the command. Then, by repetition you cement it all in his think-tank. Along the way in his training he'll try you for size to see what he can get away with. This is also part of learning.

Teaching a puppy is just like a kid building with blocks. The kid builds block by block until the whole thing falls down because of a mistake. So he starts over from the beginning, eventually learning that he can build higher by making the foundation stronger. So the puppy learns: first SIT, then STAY, then COME. When he goofs on COME start him over with SIT, then STAY. He'll finally learn COME, but in the meantime the repetition of the things he knows, SIT and STAY, makes them firmly understood upstairs.

The good part about all this training is that the trainer doesn't have to be smart. I've seen some rather sad humans train some smart dogs. It's not like teaching a kid geometry — to teach that you have to be able to do it yourself. To teach a dog to fetch you don't have to be able to do it, and if you're an adult and you do, you're going to look rather foolish.

THE TEACHING ROLE

"Beware of Dog" signs should be taken seriously by trespassers and trainers. A smart dog will take advantage of the teacher. A dog is just as keen at "feeling out" in a training situation as you ought to be. He knows that he's supposed to react to the lessons with the wag of the tail. He's quick to try putting on a sad look, a put-on pose, hoping that you'll melt and stop the lesson. If you do he's got you and he'll start training you. He's just hoping that you'll decide that he's a sensitive puppy. I've seen so many dogs go untrained because the owner got the feeling the puppy wasn't mature enough for schooling. People forget that learning is never easy and the only way to be successful as a trainer is to keep the pupil-teacher relationship rigid while school is in session. Always win your point while training; you must retain the authority at all times. The way is easy; if you use firmness sprinkled with affection, the dog will soon learn that he can't evade his lessons.

Handling the dog at such an early age is the key to the new training method. *Early training automatically makes the learning process a way of life for the dog.*

HOW TO BUILD CONFIDENCE

A dog has to learn to have confidence in you. We began to earn the confidence of the puppy when we took him out of his litter at seven weeks of age. The trainer is now the mother, and as mother you have the opportunity and the responsibility of molding the desired personality in the dog. This is one of the main reasons for taking the dog from the litter at seven weeks.

As the training schedule begins, the dog will respond to the trainer's demands. It's important here to be consistent. Don't be changeable. Make sure the dog knows what's expected of him and of you or you'll undermine all the good you have accomplished by starting early.

Dogs are very practical and have no moral sense. They'll use any method that will achieve what *they* want. Children will do the same thing. If a dog learns that he can get what he wants by whimpering and whining, he'll do it. If he gets the attention he needs by barking, he'll bark. It's very important to teach a dog from the beginning that there's a right and a wrong way to do things. The right way will get him your pleasure. If he insists on doing things the wrong way, make darn sure that he knows that he's heading for trouble.

To continue to build confidence throughout the training, make sure the dog knows what was expected of him in the particular situation before you reprimand him. Make sure he knows why he's being punished. A young dog has practically no memory, so you have to be Johnny-on-the-spot with the reprimand. Simple lapses can shatter confidence.

Developing confidence in retrievers is most essential to training. We've stated before that a retriever must *believe in you* to do his job. This is confidence.

I was mighty impressed the first time I saw a dog's absolute belief in the handler demonstrated. The dog was a Golden. The handler gave the dog a line. He was being sent across an open area of Long Island Sound. This was not a field trial. Duck season wasn't on. No shot had been fired. The dog had no idea of what was out there. He was just commanded to go. And go he did. He swam as straight as an arrow. He swam and swam and swam. He never checked back to see if the handler had gone nuts. He swam until he started to look a little small out there. As he passed an island an assistant, who had been sent there previously to hide, threw a dummy ahead of the dog. The dog never saw the thrower, but that's not important. The important thing to that dog was that he knew if he followed instructions of his handler it would lead him to his reward . . . an object to retrieve.

During training, if the dog seems to be confused, stop the lesson and start over. Say nothing, just start over. Make sure you're not expecting too much. Make sure the dog understands you. Shorten the test.

Don't try to send your dog 200 yards for a blind retrieve before he learns to go 15 yards, then 25 yards, and so on. Once he understands what's expected he can be extended.

Build the confidence at 15 or 25 yards and you'll get the work at 200 yards. Build confidence with reward step by step in all phases of the training, right from age 7 weeks.

SOME WORDS ABOUT REPRIMAND

Let's face it. If you're going to train a dog for the field you're going to have to reprimand the critter. If you're one who believes that a dog should not be spanked, you'd better stop reading right here and get yourself a book on photography or basket weaving.

There's a wide difference between dog lovers and dog trainers. A trainer accomplishes two things — loves his dog and has a well-behaved working companion. Lovers of dogs can accomplish only one thing. Affection alone produces spoiled brats and unmanageable dogs . . . discipline by the hand on the rump can be an act of love.

The major problem that the beginning trainer has to face is that when he doesn't know what else to do he spanks the dog. The man who really learns to train is the fellow who can figure out the situation and approach the problem from a different angle. Pounding on a dog proves one thing: that the trainer is bigger than the dog. If the desire to please is developed in the dog from an early age, when you come to a place in the training where things just don't seem to be going right, there can be a few reasons for this.

The dog just doesn't know what's expected of him. For example, many young dogs will drop their bird when they come out of the water, shake, and then pick up the bird again and deliver to hand. The inexperienced handler will charge at the dog when he comes back to shore and drops the bird, screaming for him to HOLD! HOLD! This just produces high blood pressure on the trainer's part and confusion on the dog's part. It's so much simpler to start running away from the dog as he hits the shore, call his name, clap your hands, blow the come-in whistle trill . . . all the excitement will make him forget to shake. He'll come a-running to you.

Another system: work the dog at first from water's edge. Let him learn you want hand delivery. Then gradually step back a yard at a time. If he drops, start back at water's edge. He'll learn delivery to hand is part of the game.

Also, a common error that leads to frustration with the inexperienced trainer is that he sets up tests that are hard for the dog. He doesn't recognize what the dog has really learned, he extends the dog too far on a command and both the dog and trainer are in trouble. Remember, a dog does not reason with his learning as a child does.

Teach a child two and two are four and he'll learn it. Then ask the child how many apples he would have if he had two in one hand and two in the other and the child will answer four apples.

Teach a dog to take a cast to the right by hand signal and have him find the bird at 15 yards will be one thing, but to try to extend him to 50 yards will only end up as rotten apples.

If a dog follows a command once that doesn't mean he has learned the command. It must be repeated and repeated until habit takes over for his lack of reasoning power.

This is an extremely important fact about training retrievers, and the trainer *must* recognize it. Most old-time trainers confuse this point with what they call "taking a dog too fast."

I distinguish between taking a dog too fast and taking a dog too far.

An eager six-month-old retriever can be taught hand signals for simple retrieves. So, if he can learn it and love doing it he's not being taught too fast. The trouble comes when the tests are made too hard too fast.

Let me put it this way. A child is taught his ABC's, then taught to read the word *cat*. When he's in the sixth grade he isn't given a refresher course in his ABC's.

A dog is taught his ABC's and then taught to make a relatively complicated retrieve. When he's six years old and is being primed for a field trial, he *is* given a refresher course in his basic ABC's.

To train a retriever successfully, make the tests simple. Gradually increase the difficulty of the tests, but frequently go all the way back to the simple tests.

Another reason for things going wrong has to do with the age of the dog. Dr. Scott's research shows that the dog goes through a period of expressing his independence. Kids go through these phases, too. The scientists show that the first time this happens is during the sixteenth and seventeenth weeks. Trainers note that it happens again at about age eight months and again at two years of age. During these periods the dog knows damn right well what is expected of him, but in his way he's trying you out to see if he can show you who's going to be the boss. That's the time to prove who's going to run this shop.

This doesn't mean that the command NO will be used only during these periods of his development. Not by a long shot. These specific periods are pointed out so that the trainer will understand that they are a normal expression of the dog's development, and you should be ready for them.

From the moment the dog enters his new home with you, he's going to hear one command and he'll continue to hear it the rest of his life. . . . It's the command NO. The whole purpose of training is to diminish the use of this command. By the time the puppy is an adult, he'll know what's expected of him and the command will very seldom be necessary.

Reprimand can take many forms and degrees. It doesn't mean only the act of laying a leash across his back. You can hurt a dog just as much by completely ignoring him. For example, if you're teaching him STAY and instead he COMES, he'll expect a pat and a kind word. Don't give him the time of day. Take him back to where he was; start him over. Ignoring him hurts his pride.

A dog instinctively recognizes a threatening gesture. If you're sure that he knows what's expected but suspect that he's just ignoring you, come at him with an upraised hand. Here's where you have to use your judgment. Consider the degree of the offense; if it is not a thrashing offense I usually use my hat as the threatening weapon. This approach will make him fold . . . he'll come around. Take into account the circumstances, the age of the dog, and whether he should have known better — then mete out the punishment.

When he becomes downright ornery and stubborn, there's only one way to straighten him out. Heaven protect me from the SPCA, but I'm going to say it. Thrash the dog. Do it with fervor, but with intelligence. I clip the dog with the folded leash until he cries out once. I talk angrily and make a big fuss while I swing, and continue to speak in a firm tone after the outcry to be sure it registered. Then I switch over to a pleasant tone of voice and begin the lessons all over again. It's very important to get the situation back to normal as quickly as possible. Don't nag. This clean-cut discipline isn't cruel, as some think. It's kind. Failure to discipline is crueler.

LET'S TALK

Dogs become masters at interpreting sound of voice or whistle. They never understand our language as we know it; they work mainly from the tone of the words. You can scold a dog by harshly telling him you love him. A dog has very sensitive ears and he's irritated by harsh, high-pitched tones. Keep your voice down in low conversational tones. The tone can encourage a puppy, but don't beg a dog to respond to a command. There's no place for baby talk in training. It's a command you're giving, not a request, so speak with authority.

A dog may try you out by puttering around before he starts to respond to your command. He's just stalling for time and trying to see how much he can get away with. Show him with a good rousing *"Hey you! What's going on?"* It'll straighten him out.

There are only about ten words that your dog's going to learn, but he'll learn hundreds of intonations.

The commands should be short, brisk, single words like SIT, STAY, COME, NO. Don't add a lot of gibberish to the commands. Don't say, "SIT boy, come on now . . . SIT, fellow . . . no, no, let's try it again. Over here now, Beau, SIT." A dog's just going to get confused with all your complicated language. In that example, we were asking the dog to do one thing — SIT . . . but if you go back over that language you'll see that four commands were given — SIT, NO, COME, BEAU. His name is really a command for attention.

Man has the ability to hear what is spoken and enlarge upon it. We call this reading between the lines. Kids learn quickly how to answer with part of the facts to convey a certain impression. Diplomats do the same thing. Man-to-man communication is a very complicated "science." We spend our lifetimes learning the game.

As far as dogs are concerned, communications are literal. No means NO. SIT means SIT. There are no shadings or interpretations. The only question that can arise in a dog's think-tank once he knows the commands is if you really mean it!

If the dog is close by, the first command should be soft but firm. If you get no action, raise the voice. If you have to tell him the third time, let your neighbors hear it.

In spite of thousands of years of domestication, dogs still have retained most of their primeval instincts; man has lost most of his. Man has come to depend on language for most of his communication; dogs use all their senses. I've heard an old dog trainer say, "One thing dogs and women have in common: they know your true feelings, no matter what you say." A dog will instinctively try to sense your attitude, and respond accordingly. He'll learn your every gesture, your expression. It's said that if you're afraid, a dog can smell your fear.

YOUR STANCE AND MOVEMENTS

In conducting the lessons, how you look to the dog is important. Your body movements and position will influence the dog's response. Your movements should be slow and deliberate, never quick and jerky. Never rush at the pup to make a correction. Move in slowly and start the lesson all over.

Your body position can make the difference between just doing what he is told and doing it with enthusiasm. The pictures show this. The upright stance does not appear to the dog to be as friendly a position. You command COME and he will obey — but, bend over and he'll come — a-running. He'll respond with enthusiasm. Even a puppy understands this. From across the room or yard, say nothing to the pup; sit down, watch him run to you.

Since a dog can't really understand your language, he uses all kinds of aids to understand you. Ever notice when you approach a strange dog, if you put your hand out from a standing position he'll be cautious? If you bend over and meet him on his own level, he'll lick your face. Standing over a dog is a threat to him. In the early schooling period, bend over, show him you're a friend.

We have already mentioned that the dog learns many things on the unconscious level. The basic training of the commands is done with the voice. Hand signals and the whistle come into play as reinforcements for the voice. By repetition the dog associates the voice command with the supporting signal. With no effort on your part he'll unconsciously learn the supporting signal as a substitute for the voice. Right from the beginning of the formal lessons the signals that reinforce the voice should be used.

The stance you take while giving voice commands with hand signals is

Standing upright does not appear as a friendly attitude to a dog. He'll come reluctantly.

YOUR STANCE AND MOVEMENTS

important. When you drive your car to town, the cop at the intersection raises his hand, palm out toward you: he reinforces the command by blowing his whistle; you stop. But either the upraised hand or the whistle alone would have you automatically reaching for your brake. I'm not suggesting that you have your dog drive you to town. I'm merely trying to show you that your dog learns to respond exactly the way you do — same mechanism.

START 'EM YOUNG...WITH THE RIGHT HABITS

Planning the habits that are going to become the adult dog's way of life is important right from the beginning. You should decide right from the beginning what house manners you're going to allow your dog to have. If you want him up on the furniture, sleeping on the beds or begging from the table, let him start that way as a pup. If you have other ideas, take the extra work out of learning — develop good habits early.

While on the subject of house manners, the old theory that you'll ruin a hunting dog by keeping him in the house was thought up by some old housewife who hated dogs. A dog that lives with people will learn faster, and the smells of the house will not ruin his nose for hunting.

As noted earlier, some trainers feel that the most frequent error amateur trainers make is to start the dog too young in obedience or field training. I've heard the statement often, "Let the puppy get dry behind the ears before you expect him to do a day's work." I couldn't disagree more. When we take a puppy home and play retrieve with him the first few days he's in the "big new kennel," we're already starting the training. From then on we'll take that pup step by step, always directing his play and his lessons toward his adult job . . . to be a retriever. We can, as you will see, accomplish a lot in those first few months.

Bend over and show him that you are his friend. Call him by name and he'll show spunk...

...Clap your hands and keep calling. As soon as he gets the idea switch over to the...

...whistle instead of the voice. But be careful he does not shove it down your throat.

People all agree that pups can be housebroken or taught other things that are against their basic nature at an early age. They seem to separate those things that are for *their* convenience and those that are for the dog's good.

If a dog can be trained to be housebroken, he can be trained to all his simple commands. Why wait?

Let me give what I consider a perfect example. I cannot claim that there is scientific fact for this example as Dr. Scott can for his mental-development theories because I have never had an opportunity to try this test on a large number of dogs. But it has worked on all the pups I have handled, and I feel sure my theory would stand up under the test of what educators or statisticians would call a random sample.

I put a pup into the home environment on the 49th day. I take the place of his mother, and all his needs are fulfilled. He starts to learn immediately. He learns where his bed is. He learns the noise his pan makes when supper is being prepared. He learns that my wife seems to be the one who handles food around this "kennel." In a few days he even learns in which cabinet the dog food is kept and what other animals around the house like to play and those that don't. For argument's sake, let's label this *self-directed learning*. My wife, who is a graduate student in sociology, gave me that term. I just wanted to get this on the record so my hunting buddies wouldn't think I was going off my rocker.

Self-directed learning is the learning the dog does which fills his own needs. These needs come from within.

Trainer-directed learning is just what it says. The dog learns something that the trainer wants it to learn, such as command SIT, STAY, and so on.

The interesting thing that I have observed is that a very young puppy will learn on the self-directed level only. Then there will be *one day* when this changes and the pup will recognize and start to accept trainer-directed learning. This has proved to be such an interesting phenomenon that I feel it worth more than just a mention. Here's how it worked with Jock and Tar, the dogs used in the pictures for this book. You'll see what advantage this will be to the retriever trainer.

They were both brought into the home on the 49th day. They became acclimated to the new surroundings and learned all sorts of things on the self-directed level.

Let me use Jock as the example. He learned where his bed was, which corner of the kitchen was the bathroom. He learned how to ask for water, and within a week learned how to open the cabinet and raid the dog-food bag. He learned that the old poodle, our house pet, wanted no part in playing with a rambunctious pup.

He learned everything about his home, the kitchen, even to stay away from the oven when it was in use. His learning was of the self-satisfying and self-protective nature. He learned what he wanted to learn. But he would respond to nothing that I wanted him to learn. If I put a leash on him he bucked. Any effort I made to teach him command SIT met with no success. If I tried to get his attention, he responded only if he wanted to. He didn't respond to his name. This, you will see, will be the key to his passing from the self-directed to the trainer-directed learning.

Every evening Jock was allowed out of the kitchen for a short play period. He explored the living room with great interest. He found all sorts of fascinating things to play with. Every night while he played I sat across the room, and when he was energetically playing with the cat, a toy, the kids or a bone I called his name in a sharp tone of voice. His name would be called only once while he was deeply engrossed at play and facing away from me. He ignored my voice in spite of the fact that he responded to his name while being fed or played with.

This little test was continued every evening. Then one evening when his name was called he momentarily stopped playing when I called, looked my way, then went back to his game.

When Jock first responded to this type of situation, he was sixty-eight days old. This response was my signal that he was ready for his first trainer-directed learning, and here's what happened.

I put a leash and collar on him. He didn't buck. I commanded SIT and showed him what I meant by that command. This will be shown to you later in pictures. He responded. Within a period of three minutes he got the idea. I stopped the lesson. An hour later I tried him again on command SIT. He remembered. Next morning before I went to work he did the job fine. That evening he sat without any assistance from my left hand. Next morning I added one more step. I commanded SIT and blew one blast on the whistle. The next day I reversed this and blew the whistle first, then commanded SIT. He responded. Next day he sat on one blast. There was no need to use the voice command after that. The whistle became his language. Within a week this play game became one of the most useful tools in retriever training. He sat at any time, off the leash, no matter what he was doing, when he heard one blast of the whistle. At eleven weeks of age the command was solidly established upstairs.

It took only three days to teach the command SIT and convert it from voice to whistle. A few more days made it solid. Within a week after that, he learned COME by voice and then whistle.

The experience with Tar was the same except he went from the self-directed to the trainer-directed learning on the seventy-first day.

Everyone thought it was cute to see such young puppies romping in a field and have the whistle commands sprung on them and see such sure-fire response. This was not just a game in my way of training, as we shall see later. The dog learns, from the earliest moment, that the whistle is the trainer's way of talking to him.

Recognizing that there are two forms of learning, self-directed and trainer-directed, will be important all through the schooling. It's only natural that a dog will want to slip back to the self-directed even after he learns what the trainer wants.

SOME MORE THINGS

The first thing that seems to pop into the noggins of people who see one of my young retrievers work is that I must be overworking them to get the kind of response from them that I do. Some people have gotten furious and told me I'm ruining the dog; others are more polite and ask how often and how long I train.

The length of time is a hard one to answer. I don't do it by the clock, I do it by the tail. A high tail means let's keep going, a low one means . . .

ANTICIPATE THE MOVE

Take the frustration out of training. Command SIT, STAY. Move back, repeat command STAY. If he decides to come, quickly command COME. Now he's done two things right, nothing wrong.

O.k., Boss, school is over. The weather has a lot to do with it. Keep it short when it's hot and muggy.

Learn to anticipate how the dog is going to respond and what the dog is going to do.

I've driven my dogs as far as twenty miles, started training with dummies and had them back in the car and driving home in a matter of five minutes. They just weren't "with me," and it was just easier on me and on them not to force the issue.

In yard training a pup, anticipating what the pup is going to do will take a lot of the frustration out of the work for both of you. For example, when a pup is held by command in the SIT, STAY position, he, of course, will want to break and come to you. After he has held it for a short period, but just can't stand it any longer, he'll give a warning by a slight body movement that he's about to break. Anticipate this — command COME just before he breaks. Now he has done two things correctly instead of one thing incorrectly. The lesson continues in a happy mood.

If you're going to train two dogs in elementary phases, or if you're going to train with a friend who has a young, inexperienced dog, don't train them simultaneously. This is important. I've seen good dogs turned into nervous wrecks under conditions that can get loud and maybe a little rough. The theory that one dog will learn from seeing another work "just ain't so" in the beginning stages. Reprimanding one young dog in front of another makes them both cringe. The dog that is sitting and watching the other one work will not be able to understand the harsh voice or the spanking, but he will react. The only time they should be worked together is when one of the dogs is calmly being taught to honor. But when this is being taught, the dog that is being honored should be sure of his job so that the problem of his reprimand just won't come up.

Train in an area where you'll have no distractions. Kids or other dogs can disrupt the classroom.

A young pup needs a lot of praise and affection as he learns his lessons. As the dog gets older the work itself will be his reward. I overheard some visitors at a field trial express amazement that after the dog had completed a long, difficult job the handler didn't praise the dog or even give him a pat. It's hard for people to understand that the greatest reward the dog would really want is to do the job all over again. They're bred to do this work, and the bird is his paycheck. This reward, the bird, will become an important training tool, as you will see later.

Don't train by the stomach; train in the head. Tidbits make the bowels work; a kind word in the ear makes his brain work. I had a friend who gave his hunting dog a dog bone every time he completed a good job. That was soon stopped. It seems that one day when they were sitting in a duck blind a pair of blacks came in to stool. *Bang! Bang!* and there were two dead ducks. Gig was sent on his way to bring in the meat. He did a fine job. The boss worked through his layers of clothing to find the milk bones. Just as he reached them, another pair of ducks swung into the decoys. He reloaded his gun but never got it to his shoulder. In his excitement to reload, he shoved the dog biscuits into his double.

TRY HIM ... SPRING COMMAND

Get him used to the idea that commands are to be obeyed, no matter when they are given. Start him early at this game. Spring commands when you are playing indoors or out. But do not overdo on this. There is nothing worse than a trainer who won't give a dog any peace. Tar, age fourteen weeks, and I were playing chase. In the middle of the game I sprung command SIT, and he did it, fast.

ONE LAST WORD

You do not start to train a dog by getting a dog. The first step is to lie down on a couch and get a few things straight.

First thing, ask yourself if you have patience. Be honest in answering. If you answer No, that's a good start.

The most important trait you need to be a successful trainer is to be logical. You'll have to train a dog step by step. You'll have to know the steps and recognize when the next step can be made. Most trainers go too slow, and that is where this book will differ from the standard retriever training book.

The logic of the training will be set forth for you. That's what this book is about. To go with it, you'll have to be consistent in the training. To be consistent, you must understand the purpose of each step and see to it that both you and the dog follow them.

The best way to train is to build confidence. Some train by fear, and do a successful job. In my opinion, the same thing can be achieved by firmness and consistency at the correct time.

Can you be the boss? This is important. If you can't transmit authority by the way you handle yourself and the way you use your voice, you might as well just put this dog in a show ring and forget the idea of using him as a worker.

A boss in training a dog is different than a boss in the business world. The boss in the office knows that he can get more out of people by making requests of people. The authority for the request comes in the form of a paycheck at the end of the month.

Remember, a dog trainer never makes a request of a dog. He commands a dog.

This dog is going to be a retriever. The course of his training should be in that one direction. Don't bother to fill his head with all sorts of parlor tricks. Rolling over and playing dead is what the ducks are supposed to do, not your dog.

What do we want in this dog?

He's going to have to be an eager worker. His drive to retrieve must be as strong as his desire to eat. He has to be pliable, take directions, and yet be a driver. If you command him to go through muck, he should do it with heart. A retriever is a servant, almost a slave, but he will have a dignity and will command respect. You'll never have a better friend.

How do we get all this in one dog? Read on.

Part II

Chapter 4

Kindergarten — Molding the Retriever for Work

I'll work my retrievers at the drop of a hat; they're pretty good at re-trieving hats, too. One day (when my hat was off) and I was working the dogs, a man who was watching finally got up nerve to come over and talk to me. I guess he was afraid at first that one of us might bite. He was amazed at what the dogs could do, but the thing that bothered him was *How do you start, where do you start, when do you start?*

There's no more graphic way of showing the training theory we've dis-cussed in Part I than with photographs — except, perhaps, if you have a friend who has successfully trained a retriever and is willing to show you the path and its pitfalls.

We've previously mentioned that we were going to give you a new training tool for the job. That tool is the Retriev-R-Trainer and we'll discuss it at length later, but for now, let me say the research and development of this gadget was much like dog training.

The end product is the important thing; minor details can become the confusing issues. A working retriever is the end product. Whether he is trained to heel on your right or left side is a minor detail. You are going to have to play the part of the researcher to see what details work best for you and your dog. Right-handed people like the dog on the left to keep the dog out of the way of the gun, yet many right-handed people like the dog on the right because they can control the dog better with their more skilled hand and arm. Throughout the pictures I show you what I do. . . . Take the minor details for what they're worth. Change them if you wish to fit your needs. What I'm trying to sell here is the overall plan. If you don't believe it after you have read it, throw the book away; but if you think it has merit it will mean that first you will start training the dog at a much earlier time than has been suggested in the past.

Half of your battle is won by starting the dog in his training at the beginning of the fourth critical period of his mental development. If handled properly at this time the dog will be prepared to accept learning as a way of life; a cooperative dog is a most important factor in achieving the end product . . . a working retriever.

Scientists have discovered by intelligence tests that no one particular breed of dog or any one dog in a litter is smarter than any other. What they've found is this: the dog that takes responsibility faster learns better. And taking responsibility has to be learned.

The puppy starts kindergarten at seven weeks of age. For the next five weeks he gets this preschool training.

During the first five weeks of kindergarten we'll put him in the right environment and develop a sense of security. The mild restrictions and irritations that we impose on him will be to develop his tolerance. We'll set up play games, and we'll teach him specific simple commands, but most important will be the human contact he'll get during this whole period. During this preschool time we're molding the personality of the dog, we're building the foundations of a well-balanced dog.

Experimental evidence proves, as you have already read, that the optimum time to establish this essential bond between man and dog is the initial seven- to twelve-week period. It's interesting to note that before this time dogs show a fear response toward man. But by the time the dog is 49 days old his fears become wants that increase his need for contact with man. For example, don't run down to the kitchen in your flannel nightgown at 3 A.M. to quiet the new yelping puppy. Overnight isolation of the pup increases his fear and anxiety and reinforces the bond between trainer and dog the next morning: "Absence makes the heart grow fonder."

Some trainers have the idea that every time a puppy yelps he's hungry, so they feed him, thinking this is what the pup needs and the youngster will love him more if he keeps his belly full. Not so, say the scientists. Mild hunger pains tend to speed the bond between man and his hungry friend.

I mention these findings just to show that there are some new ways of thinking about some old facts we thought we knew. Some of the training methods are going to be new, too, so don't be surprised.

We'll start from the beginning and show in pictures how to go about training, and in words what each step means.

Feed him. Care for him and take the part of Mother and you'll have a secure pup who will play by himself and "attack" anything that wants to play with him. Insecurity? Boot it.

SECURITY — DUCKLINGS GET IT FROM DUCKS RETRIEVERS GET IT FROM YOU

In preparing him to learn to retrieve a duck *your way*, the first step is to make him secure.

Dog breeders and trainers are often heard to say, "Oh, a fine puppy, very well bred, but a little sensitive." Sensitive, hell. That pup is insecure; it's scared to death of its own shadow. Trainers will also talk of strongheaded pups that need a firm hand. Secure dogs neither have to win battles nor be afraid. Sensitive or hardheaded dogs are undesirable; in either case the dogs became what they were through their litter experiences or something in the training does it — they weren't born that way. Both cases can be avoided.

It's obvious that in the first case the sensitive puppy lived too long with its litter mates and was beaten up too often; in the second case the headstrong puppy or the bully was the pup that won all the fights in the litter.

We now know why dogs develop different personalities. By removing the pup from its litter at seven weeks and then providing him with all his needs, protecting him from harm, making the new home a pleasant one, we'll make him a secure puppy. A secure puppy is a happy pup. A happy puppy will take to his lessons easily.

HUMAN CONTACT — NOW OR NEVER

Strangely enough, ducks teach us much about a retriever's early behavior patterns. Retrievers are born with the instinct to retrieve, but this instinct has to be channeled by the trainer. Ducks are born with the instinct to follow. It's most startling to see ducklings follow the first object they see move after they are hatched. If it be their mother, they'll follow her anywhere. If a block of wood on a string or a person walking slowly is substituted for the mother, the ducklings will march behind and follow. If the mother duck is brought back into the picture once the ducklings have followed another object, they won't heed her.

This demonstrates that early patterns and associations imprint a definite way of future life. For the dog, to develop his natural instinct an extra factor is necessary — the trainer. Much the same as the duck, the dog at this early age forms strong bonds. It's essential in the dog's training that the handler get into the act between this seventh and twelfth week.

Until the dog comes home with you, his main contacts have been with the bitch and his litter mates. A pup at this age will form natural attachments to the one who cares for him and instructs him. Emotional development of the pup is linked with his physical and mental growth. Whoever takes the place of the mother will become very important to the dog. You should be the one who feeds the puppy. Dogs left in the kennel four or five months without real human contact will never develop to their full potential as hunting companions.

Play with your new pup often. It's not just fun, but an important part of the early learning process. It sets the stage for a good relationship. You can actually start the retrieving instinct as soon as he can walk. It's a game, he'll love it. Caution, don't overdo.

Caution, don't let the kids overdo. They have to learn the dog has rights, too. Kids can be unkind and not really mean it. Teach them that a dog's tail is not his leash, and the friendly wag of the tail has to be earned.

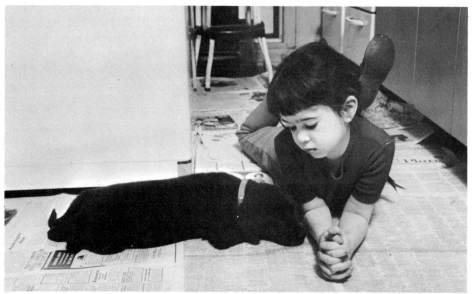

47

At meal time pup was always underfoot. He wanted to play, Mother wanted to work. This mild restriction teaches him he doesn't get his way no matter how much he jumps, whines, or barks to get free. Might as well lie down, take it easy. That's what a tied leash means.

IT'S A TOUGH LIFE

Life isn't a bed of roses, and the sooner the pup learns this, the easier it's going to be to train him. It's important that the dog develop neither a sensitive nor a soft personality. While he's going through this important development period, mild irritations and restrictions mixed with affection will teach him that life's not too bad in spite of things like a collar and a leash. I don't like a necktie any better than he likes the collar, but I have to wear one to the office. Most husbands get used to the leash and are lost without it. Start the dog with a collar a few hours at a time. Let him drag the leash around a short time each day.

At nine or ten weeks you can start to teach him command QUIET. This is going to be important later on. A dog that whines or yaps while sitting in a duck blind is a real nuisance. Such noises will not only cause ducks to flair from the stool, but your hunting buddies as well.

A dog that is not prepared for learning, by being put through necessary yet unpleasant experiences, will tend to show fear when he is confused by later lessons.

I have a friend who brought such a problem to me. He said his dog is so bad about this that when he raises his voice at the kids the dog folds and rolls on his back with fear. He said he can't understand this, since he had never so much as laid a hand on this dog. The answer seems obvious. He never required a thing of this dog for the first few months. The dog loved it.

He ate and slept and did what he wanted when he wanted. Then one day the trainer decided it was time to start to work. Of course this dog was confused. All learning has a certain amount of not understanding attached to it.

The pup that rolls over just gives up. The trainer thinks the pup is a sensitive dog, and goes easy on him, and the dog learns that if he rolls on his back the trainer will stop the lesson. Once this pattern develops the trainer's in trouble. The dog has him licked. It takes a lot of patience and skill to bring such a dog around. Every smart mother prepares her child for school. We should do the same for our dogs.

Then again there is the other side of the coin. The dog that goes through this period having his own way may learn that he can bull his way around. He's not as tough to teach as the back roller, but he's also a problem.

Teaching a pup to accept certain restrictions at this time will keep him from becoming a spoiled brat. All training is restrictive in nature. If he learns this early, half your battle is won. You as a trainer give the commands when you see fit. A working dog must do what you say when you say it. Here in preschool, early training must include learning restraint. There are two ways to teach it. One, put the puppy into a situation where he finally teaches himself; two, he learns the taboos by discipline and mild punishment. He'll want to please you so much that you'll be surprised how fast he'll get the idea.

The whole thing is just this simple. We take the pup out of the litter before he develops traits that would interfere with learning. During this five-week period when learning is so rapid, it's up to the trainer to develop the correct learning attitude, and thus take a major problem out of training. A cooperative dog will save time and headaches later.

"You know better!" This is one restriction that we insist he learn NOW! "Outside you." Command **QUIET.** Squeeze his snout. Press his jowl against his teeth. Roughly repeat **QUIET.**

These two pictures were taken a day or so apart. Left, he's self-directed. He wants no part of the leash or the trainer. As discussed on page 36, practically overnight he becomes trainer-directed. Instead of bucking you, he responds. Now he's ready for the play lessons.

KINDERGARTEN PLAY LESSONS

Once the dog demonstrates that he is ready for trainer-directed learning, you can start the simple play lessons. The dog will be about nine weeks old. These lessons are just what we say they are — play lessons. That means plenty of reward and no punishment, no matter what happens. It's not only a matter of what he learns; it's also a matter of liking the idea of school. But I've never seen a puppy yet that didn't learn all his ABC's on a leash by the time he was ready for real lessons at the age of twelve weeks.

What can you expect to teach between seven and twelve weeks? To walk fairly well at HEEL, and to know the commands SIT, STAY, and COME. He'll have learned that the leash means control; he'll have to do the things expected of him — when it's on he can't get away. It'll all be rather confusing to him at first, but when you put the leash on and give him commands he'll be getting plenty of love and attention, and that's good; he'll like it.

Command SIT is one of the most important commands for the working retriever. Not only is he required to sit at your side while waiting in a blind, but he will take his initial directions for the retrieve from a sitting position at HEEL. In "college," when he learns to handle, he'll take your directional signals while sitting at a distance from you.

I teach a puppy the SIT command first by voice. When he understands it I immediately add the whistle . . . one blast. In a few days you can drop the voice command and use only the whistle. A dog doesn't really care what "language" you use; he'd learn the command if the action of the command was associated with a bagpipe. Later we'll show how sitting on the whistle, in a very young dog, will help you make important corrections in the field. You'll be able to stop him when you see he's about to make a mistake.

Here's the way you do it. Walk the dog on a very short leash at your side. Command SIT. Pull his head up with the leash. With your other hand push his fanny down. Command SIT again when he's settled. In short order you'll have only to touch his hindquarters and he'll sit. When he'll do it without the use of the pushing hand, introduce the whistle. Command SIT. When he does it . . . blast once. In a few days reverse the order. Blast once . . . command SIT. Shortly thereafter forget the voice command.

STAY is also taught on the leash. The picture shows the correct stance. The traffic-cop signal is given and the command is repeated sharply.

COME is a command that will be extremely important in field work. If

In one day he'll learn what the command SIT means. In three days, with a little help he will know that the whistle command for sit is one sharp blast. Teach the commands by the voice, then switch to the whistle. The whistle becomes his language right from the start.

he has overrun a downed bird, you'll want him to come toward you to pick it up. But it will be important in the training also that he come in to you when you see he is about to make a mistake. You can stop him by whistle; now you may want to bring him in and start the lesson over. So, at this young age I teach the command COME by voice and then immediately teach it by whistle . . . why wait 'til he's older?

Teach it on leash at this age. Command COME; give the six-foot-long training leash a tug. A continual rolling, inviting trill is blown after the voice command is given. Once again the voice command can soon be forgotten.

When do we use the voice at all? The whistle is for the field. The voice will be used in everyday situations around the home. This brings up the subject of manners. They should be taught now. All dogs have to learn their place. This is the time to teach him to bother people, beg from the table, jump up on guests, sleep on your bed, if those are the things you want him to do. If not, you'd better show him at this age what you want and be consistent about your demands. Manners and the problems of man and dog living together and corrections are all discussed in *Family Dog;* no use wasting this space on those problems.

THAT WAS KINDERGARTEN

That was kindergarten. The lessons have just started. He's learned all sorts of things. During this time we had him travel in his Kennel-Aire in the car. He might as well learn to travel and love it, because he'll never retrieve any ducks in your living room. We took him for walks in town as soon as he could wobble along on the leash so he would learn that strange noises and things aren't going to hurt him. A spooky dog who is afraid of strangers, new situations, and places makes a tough training problem.

We've taught him the command KENNEL. It's simple. Sit him in front of the kennel door; give the command and gently shove him in; repeat the command as he goes. In a few days you won't have to shove, especially if you throw a dog biscuit in ahead of him so his belly will have something to do while he waits to be let out.

Oh, yes! Did I mention the command NO? No need to explain it. He's heard it from the moment he became your friend. Its use will diminish in

A pup should learn manners early. He's not to be the center of attention all the time.

direct relationship with your ability as a trainer.

As we look back over our progress so far, what was the most important phase of the preschool period? There's no question about it — the play games and the socializing between the trainer and the puppy were the most important. What we've tried to do is to give the puppy a specific personality and a strong desire to learn. We've controlled the environment to produce this. We've irritated him to teach him tolerance. We've cared for him to make him feel secure. We've taught him some lessons to develop a sense of responsibility. We've spent a lot of time playing with him just to show him that we love him. . . . What more could a mother do?

LET'S SHOW WHAT WE LEARNED

By this time the dog has reached the twelfth week, SIT, STAY, COME commands are understood. At this early age the retriever has learned that commands are given in three ways: by voice, by whistle, and hand signal. (The hand signal for STAY will not be used in the field later, but it helps reinforce the voice command and prepares him for the use of the hands in giving commands later.)

Walk the dog on a short leash held in your left hand. Give the voice command to sit and blow once on the whistle. Command STAY, you step ahead of him. Show him the hand signal for stay. (Pictures continue next page)...

These commands were taught on the leash. This gave you control, since to the dog the leash meant restraint.

These commands are so important that you can hardly train a retriever without perfect response to them. Much of his work will be started from the sitting position next to you. STAY gives you the flexibility needed in the teaching situation. COME is obvious; you don't want him delivering your shot bird to someone in the next blind.

Release the pressure on the dog's collar and slowly move back repeating the STAY command. His attention span is short, don't make him wait. Move to the end of the leash. Reinforce the command with the hand signal.

Give the leash a little tug. Bend down. Command COME and trill on the whistle. When he comes in show him you are very pleased. After the third lesson you won't need the leash.

Chapter 5

School for Duck Dogs

Play lessons have now ended. Teaching now goes on the conscious level of learning, which means only that the dog will know damn right well that he's being taught. Prior to the Hamilton Station research, most trainers considered a pup of this age an infant. Now we know a twelve-week-old pup's brain has attained full adult form, but, of course, he lacks experience. The next four to six weeks are the most important training time in a dog's life. I know it's hard to believe, but this scientific study (see page 24) means that a twelve-week pup must be carefully trained to get the best out of him in the future, and the training can't be interrupted at this time.

In a few weeks the dog will try you for size to see who's going to be boss. Now's the time to let him know. The lessons themselves do not abruptly change; you just make sure he does what's expected. Step by step we will add new things. We'll build on what he knows. But remember, don't you assume what he knows; take him back to his ABC's. Even in advanced lessons, when the dog learns to do triples, take him back and have him do what you will think are simple singles. This is important in training a retriever. We'll show you how to go step by step, but you remember to go back over earlier work as we go along.

From here on out, all training will be toward one goal, a working retriever. You can't make a dog sit in a duck blind if he won't sit in your living room. There will be no rolling over, playing dead, saying prayers, begging, and so forth. That stuff is for the cocktail party. The only "cocktail" this dog will enjoy is going to be in the field. Don't clutter up his brain with any useless nonsense.

LET'S START WITH THE RETRIEVE

When do we begin? Right away!

How do we begin? Let's first take a look at the retrieving job, and you'll see how to start.

Retrieving is made up of three elements: running out to the object, picking it up and then delivering it to the trainer.

This is going to be the dog's whole job in life. If he's trained properly, it'll come to be more than his job; it'll be his life.

Many trainers feel that if a young pup will run out for a thrown object, that's all they want to see. And it's true. This is a good indication. But in the early puppy training the other end of the job, carrying an object and *delivering* it, is *most* important in the early formative weeks of learning.

If a pup learns that you like him to carry and bring things to you, there'll be no problem when you throw something out. He'll run out, get it just so he can do what you want . . . deliver.

Now, how do we begin? Retriever puppies will pick up whatever they can get in their mouths. So, most important, never discourage a pup from retrieving. This sounds like an easy demand on the trainer, but this also goes for the trainer's family.

Your attitude must be, and you must show the dog, that he is a good fellow for fetching whatever it is, be it your best pipe, gloves, mail, shoes, the kids' toys, bottles of bath oil, hairbrushes, the family cat, or silk stockings. You'll just have to learn to hold your temper. So will everybody else in the house. Take the object from him gently and praise him for being a fine retriever. It once took me six months to recover a government bond that a pup played with. Just try to tell Uncle Sam that the serial number was chewed by a dog, and you'll get $18.75 worth of paper forms to fill out before you'll get the bond replaced.

One thing is sure: a retriever pup around the house will train the kids to keep their belongings off the floor. We had one pup that used to help mother with the wash. He seemed to think it was his job to make the rounds every day collecting dirty clothes the kids and Pop used to throw helter-skelter.

The family can be of great help to you in your training. If they scold him for carrying off their choice possessions and you take him into the yard and try to teach him to bring in a dummy, he's going to be one confused pup.

I know of one retriever trainer who got into a serious training problem because of such a situation. The wife left her unmentionables over a chair each night. Every morning the dog retrieved them. She scolded and chased him all over the house. He thought it was quite a game. He'd do the same thing in a training session. He'd run out, pick up a dummy, and stand and beg you to chase him. He soon learned that a two-legged man can't catch a four-legged dog.

Eventually a puppy will learn that the dummy and only the dummy is for retrieving, but until he grows out of his puppy ways an object is an object and he's not able to distinguish the value of them.

For very young pups we always have a few midget-sized dummies around the house. Every time he delivered something we didn't want him to fetch, we quietly took it away from him and then threw the bumper for him. He was in the mood to fetch, so he'd always run across the room and bring it back.

Remember, it's good to end any training situation on a good note. Having the dummy ready in this situation will show him that this is one thing that really pleases you. Although this may not seem like a real training situation, unconsciously the dog will learn that this is what you really want. It's easier to teach him on this level of learning than having to knock it into his head later.

INSTILL THE RETRIEVING INSTINCT

The object should be light and soft. A dummy should be used just as soon as he can handle it. He's born with this instinct to retrieve, but you'll have to develop it and you can't start too soon. They love to do this with a bird wing. Call him back to you as soon as he picks it up. Learning to return isn't as instinctive as running out and picking up.

MAKE IT LOTS OF FUN

Once he gets on this game he'll carry anything around the house that he can get into his mouth. It's important that he should not be scolded for retrieving wrong things. He won't know the difference between twenty-dollar new shoes and an old slipper. Always have a dummy ready. When he brings the good shoe thank him, then throw the dummy. When he brings it back, give him plenty of praise.

Command SIT, STAY firmly. Show the signal. ...command over your shoulder, give the sign
Then start to slowly walk away. Repeat the... to stay behind you as you walk out of his...

EXTEND STAY, STAY...STAY...STAY...!

This is a good command to start training the dog off leash because he's seated. The leash means control; he can't get away. Now we have to show the dog that *you* mean control. That doesn't mean you now throw away the leash. After you put him through SIT, STAY, COME a few times on leash, try it once without. In a few days you'll be able to have him sit longer if you keep reminding him to STAY by voice. Slowly keep walking backward, away from him. Then you can try going out of sight. At about fourteen weeks he'll do this nicely, but don't overdo; a pup has a short attention span. It's not the length of time at first; it's his waiting until released that's important.

A retriever has to learn this one. It's a real pain hunting in a blind with a guy whose dog is all over the place, and it's worse on water. The dog's got to learn to stop rocking the boat. SIT . . . STAY!!!

... sight. First time only for a few seconds, ... Command STAY. Gradually increase the time
then be ready to come back into his view... you leave the yard. Fool him after a bit...

... Walk all around the house. Let him guess
where and when you'll return. Try to fool him.

HEEL...DO IT, DON'T BE ONE

A retriever walks at heel and works from a sitting position at heel. Most dogs learn this command for the convenience of the master. HEEL is a retriever's business. Decide what side you're going to work your dog; from then on, be consistent; never let him switch.

Teach HEEL on a leash and choke collar. Hold him in tight, command HEEL, slap your leg with your hand. Keep repeating the command. If he wants to be out front like the bandleader . . . yank. Pull him back, command HEEL. If he tries to walk just ahead of you, hold him there by leash; walk up to him, shortening the leash as you go. If he insists on getting in your way, give no quarter; bump him out of the way. Let him learn to walk on his feet, not yours; he's got four, you have only two. If he's a laggard or a sniffer, don't drag him forward. Talk gently to him; wait for him, and start over with a short leash. Once he knows what you expect, then get tough on him.

Start 'em young; take the strain out of it. The best tool is the long leash held short, as the pictures show.

Put him through left and right turns. Teach him to stay close yet out of

Start him as soon as he can walk on a leash to get an understanding of command HEEL. Swing the leash in front of his nose. As he gets older and tougher, get rougher, clip his snout.

your way. Change your pace. The secret is command constantly. HEEL . . . HEEL . . . HEEL . . . HEEL . . . all the time you're walking. When he's doing it well, use a pleasant tone of voice. If he's being stubborn, growl the command at him.

The way to use the choke collar is to yank if necessary; apply the pressure in quick tugs. When he's next to you, release the pressure immediately.

Don't start to teach this off leash until he's got the idea to walk with his head next to your knee.

Soon all you'll have to do is show the leash. Now he's ready, unsnap the leash and carry it.

Command HEEL.   **Blast once.**

SIT, STAY, COME BY WHISTLE

From the time he's twelve weeks old 'til he's four or five months, he should have daily training of a few minutes on these commands. Most important is the whistle. This should be his language now. You'll see later just how important it will be to his future in the field. For now, you should understand that while he's young, if he learns the whistle language at your feet where you can control him, it will be like duck soup to teach the same important commands later when he's 100 yards out in the field. If he's brought up on the whistle language, he'll know what the whistle commands mean. It's just like teaching a kid a second language. Those who learn a foreign tongue at home from birth have no trouble in school. When I took French in high school, I murdered that language so badly that I switched to Spanish. (I wrecked that one, too, in short order.)

A few tips. He's got to understand that you must be obeyed *immediately*. Not tomorrow, not next week, but *right now*. When he's in the early classes in school don't command COME if you think he's not ready to do so. By the time he's about 15 weeks he should come any time he's called.

If he's reluctant, turn and run from him, calling and whistling. If he's still reluctant, something I've never had to do, use a long rope and pull him in while commanding COME. Use a high-pitched whistle and buy a mess of them; they break, freeze, and the kids swipe them.

Command STAY.   **Repeat STAY.**

Trill COME IN whistle command.

65

The young dog that jumps up can be trained DOWN by pushing him back down by the snout.

The older dog that forgets his manners can be corrected with a swift knee to the chest.

Attach the leash to the choke collar. Run the leash under your foot. Command DOWN. Make a downward motion with your hand. Pull up on the leash and force him down to the ground.

COMMAND DOWN... MEANS TWO THINGS

Jumping on people to show affection is not permitted. Having an eighty-pound dog jump up on you while you're carrying a loaded shotgun isn't exactly one of the ten rules of safe gun handling.

I never teach command DOWN, meaning lie down, to a pointing dog or a house pet. For them this is not necessary; command SIT is enough. If they wish to lie down on the SIT command, that's their business. It's a different matter with a retriever. It's not very safe, for example, hunting brant from a layout boat with a sitting dog. You're lying on your back waiting for the birds to stool, and the only space left for the dog is between your legs. A sitting dog will get in the way of the gun when you snap to a sitting position to shoot.

There are two ways to teach lie down. The first method is so simple it requires no pictures. Sit the dog in front of you. Get down on your knees and take his front paws in your hands. Command DOWN; lift his paws, pull them toward you. Down he'll go. Keep repeating the command and then put one hand on his shoulders and hold him down.

If this doesn't work, try the pictured method. Note how unhappy Tar looks in the pictures. This method is very restrictive for a young dog.

Work him off the leash. The command is DOWN and the hand signal is a downward motion of the hand. The hand signal is quiet and makes more sense in a duck blind than a voice command.

Chapter 6

"No Name" Chapter... Just New Things

There are no such things as definite progressive chapters in training a dog. The experienced trainer is going back to early lessons and is going ahead to new things at the same time. Training is like weaving a piece of cloth; we hope that the design of the woof will add up to a duckhunting motif.

But, for your purpose, if the final design is going to include upland game, you'll have to teach your dog to quarter the field like a Springer or a Setter.

Since the retriever is going to flush the game, he'll have to work within gun range. Of course, you'll want him to hunt or quarter the field in front of you. You decide the hunting direction, not the dog.

Here's what you can expect: this is part of the unconscious learning that we've talked about. First, we teach the puppy to take his correct place, in front of the hunter. He'll learn this by habit. If you start your puppy at a very young age, he'll have a strong desire to stay very close to you. We'll take advantage of this, and on the first few walks teach him this place in the field.

Next, we'll teach him to hunt the area. As he develops more boldness and wanders farther away from you, but still has need to be near you, we teach him now to hunt or quarter.

We'll wind up by having him do all this by hand signal alone. Having implanted the habit of being in the right place and doing the right thing early in his training, before he's had an opportunity to learn anything else, he'll be way ahead of the game. He'll have nothing to unlearn. And the best part of this system is that he has learned without knowing it.

This training is started way back in kindergarten. The pup should be taken out into a field to romp and play for two reasons: to teach him it's a great big world and to teach him his place in it . . . ahead of the hunter.

More often than not a pup taken to a strange field with cover will hang on your heels. That's good; just lift your feet high as you walk and gently clip him in the jaw. He'll soon learn to stay a yard or so behind you. Then never let him behind you again. When he takes his place behind you, you turn around. Now he's in front of you. Walk on; if he gets to the side or

* *Gun Dog*, by R. A. Wolters (New York: E. P. Dutton & Co., 1961). See pages 58–65.

behind you, turn, face him. He'll learn his place . . . it's in front of you.

Of course, he'll get bolder as he learns the field is a wonderful place to be. You now walk the field in a zigzag. If you start this early, you won't have a problem because he's not bold enough yet to want to run off; he'll want you in sight.

He's learned to be in front of you and he'll want to go where you go. Walk twenty-five yards, then zig ninety degrees. If it's to the left, call his name for attention and give him an arm signal to the left and command GO ON. Walk twenty-five yards in the new direction, then zag to the right. He'll soon learn to check back to see where you're going. If not, call his name, give him a right-hand signal and walk the new direction.

After a bold pup learns this, he might have a tendency to run off and play. A smart dog will turn familiar terrain into his own backyard. Take such a dog to a new area and he won't be so bold.

Once he gets the hang of this game cut your zigs and zags down from ninety degrees to forty-five. What we want him to learn is that the appropriate hand signal means the new direction.

If he starts to get out too far as these lessons advance, the call in whistle command should be given. As he comes in, give the hand signal and zig. As you reduce the angle of zigzag and he follows the direction signals, you'll soon note that you'll be able to walk a straight line and he'll quarter by signal. Now you can send him any whichway with the hand and the GO ON commands. (See *Gun Dog.*°)

Clip the pup that hangs on your heels with your boot. He'll learn to drop back out of the way. Then you turn around. Now he's in front of you. Whichever way he turns, you turn. His place is out front. Quartering starts.

NOW WE'RE ON OUR WAY

The dog has been prepared for learning and he's been taught his basic commands. Now we start him with all kinds of experiences connected with his future job as a retriever. We teach him early to have no fear of water, boats, guns, game, decoys, and so on. Our early training taught him not to spook with people; now we want to broaden that attitude.

As an example, let's begin with water. Don't start by throwing something in for him to retrieve. I've seen young pups spook on the splash. The introduction to water should be with you. Put on a bathing suit or a pair of boots and show him you like it. Don't raise your voice if he refuses. Stop and try it next day. He'll soon walk in; try to coax him the rest of the way. Dogs don't have to be taught to swim; that comes built in as standard equipment.

Start the dog off in fresh water. A pup's likely to drink, and salt water will make him sick. Seek out a hard bottom with a gradual slope for the introduction. Deep, mucky pond edges can frighten a dog.

Walk out into the water, call him, tease him, clap your hands, blow the whistle.

For the guy who thinks you train the dog to swim by throwing him in . . . holes in his waterwings.

Be gentle with him. Soon he'll hit the water with a splash. Don't start him off retrieving before he gets his sea legs. A belly full of water can discourage a youngster. It takes a few experiences in water for him to learn to hold his head down. A pup will arch his neck and he'll swim in such a position as to make so much splash that he could swim right past a dummy and never even see it. Give him time.

Jock has been at it now a few days, so we gave him a little more difficult water entry...

MAKE SWIMMING FUN WITH A RETRIEVE

Right from the time we've had the pup, we've played retrieve with him on land. He already has an idea what the game is, so we can now let him do it in water. If he's not retrieving in the backyard, wait with the water bit, unless you're part fish. Never throw balls, sticks or any such things for your retriever to fetch. Use only training dummies and birds. I saw this happen once, I swear: we were sitting in a blind with a "good hunting dog but never trained"; a duck was crippled but down, and the dog hit the water. The duck dived, so the dog retrieved the next best thing, a floating hunk of wood. Try that on your table.

Make sure the pup thinks he's part fish before you start water retrieves. The first ones should be thrown so he has only to wade for them. Make a fuss over him and toss it into deeper water. Before he realizes it, he'll be swimming.

With the right tone of voice and attitude you can get him so excited that he'll start hitting the water with glee.

...We excited him, used short retrieves. Added new things, like water entry, one at a time.

Start him to come in by whistle from the beginning. Save the voice for praise and reprimand.

BOTTOMS UP

Don't wait until you're going to take the dog on his first hunt to get him used to a boat. The same thing goes for the car. When the dog is supposed to enter a car, command KENNEL. I use the same command for a boat.

Dogs will spook in a boat if you don't teach them young, that in spite of all the leaks "it ain't going to hurt." Get them used to the noise, the motion, and the crazy floor.

Let him explore all he wants on the first few trips. Later he'll be given his place with the command DOWN.

Get him used to an outboard motor. Docks also present a problem. Coax the reticent dog onto the open boards; use a leash; he knows that means control.

I know one hunter who couldn't get his dog onto a dock, let alone into a boat. He solved the whole thing in a few days. He put the dog's food on the dock first. His stomach got up the courage for him. Next day the food was placed in the boat. Again his stomach taught him to walk down the dock, jump in the boat, and eat.

Once he has sea legs, throw a dummy for him. He'll dive overboard. If not, don't force him. Wait until he's worked on live shackled ducks. Then try him. Throw the duck six feet windward . . . splash!

The returning dog is the problem. Some hunters have a ramp for him to climb on. Others just take the bird from him while he's in the water. He'll try to climb in. Help him. When he hooks his front legs over the gunnel, put your hand behind his head and press down. That will give him the leverage needed to climb in.

Of course, a simpler way is to lift him in. Except when you grab him by the scruff of the neck and the tail, the "lift in" may turn into a "pull out." Hunting clothes tend to make a hunter sink.

THE BIG BOOM BOOM

Once a pup is settled and well established in the house, I always start a mealtime ritual. I shoot off a cap pistol, then immediately feed the dog. Within a week he'll start to salivate when the gun goes off. He's conditioned; loud noises now mean something good; you won't have any future worry if he's started early. Later that same noise will be associated with something as good as food . . . a bird to retrieve.

Very few retrievers show signs of gunshyness. It should take only one session to get him used to the shotgun. Have a helper at about 50 yards shoot and then throw a bird. Let the dog retrieve. Gradually the helper can move closer and closer to the dog.

People worry too much about gunshyness. Try this test. In most cases it's for you, not the dog. Have a bunch of friends shoot clay birds. Get the noise booming. Start the dog 100 yards away on leash. Walk him slowly; see if he's enjoying it or getting upset. I'll bet 100 to 1 you'll be able to walk right up with him, take a gun, and miss a few clay birds yourself. You'll be more aggravated than the dog.

Of course, as the picture shows, it didn't happen that way with me. I broke every bird in such small pieces that there was nothing for Tar to retrieve. He got bored and went to sleep.

The Dummy-Launch is a new retrieving device for the training of hunting dogs and is being made to my specifications by Turner Richards of England. It is superior in design and handling to the Retriev-R-Trainer, which I co-designed with Arthur Johnson as a training tool some twenty years ago when this book was originally published. The new Dummy-Launch offers major improvements. The handle is of heavy, flexible rubber with a shield designed to protect the hand. It helps absorb the normal kick, eliminating a firing problem. The dummies are the best ever made for dog training. There are three types and each comes either white or colored. They are practically indestructible and like no other dummies on the market. They are designed for the dog and the force of the gun and will not blow apart. These dummies can also be used with the old Retriev-R-Trainer gun. They come in semi-hard plastic, softer canvas-covered plastic, and semihard plastic balls. The 3½-inch ball is a new device to teach a dog to track. The dog sees it fly and land. The ball then rolls on. The dog goes to the mark, then has to search out its new location. He is first taught with a yellow ball, which he can see. When the dog learns the game, the black ball is used. Now the dog has to use his nose; he has to track to find it. The plastic dummy leaves the spud with enough speed for it to travel up to 100 yards. Blank .22 ammunition is the propellant, and comes in different charges: light, medium, and heavy, permitting dummy flights of from 30 yards to the maximum distance. Long flights teach the dog to track a flying object. The noise of the "gun" is built into the device. Extra dummies make it possible to put out doubles and triples. The pictures, right, show how the device is fired. The angle of the arm is important. It is shot with the right arm held across the body. The arm absorbs the force.

The Dummy-Launch, the improved Retriev-R-Trainer, can be purchased from Hallmark Blackwatch, West 250 North 8815, Hillside Road, Sussex, Wisconsin, 53089; telephone 414-246-4000.

DUMMY-LAUNCH...A NEW TOOL

On a hunting trip to Maine, I met Ted Williams. There was no better arm in baseball. Ted also has a great sense of humor, so I bet him that I could throw a training dummy three times as far as he could. Not to be outdone, Ted took me on. I gave him a boat-bumper-type training dummy, and he heaved. There's a trick to it that he didn't know, so he got only about 30 yards out of it. I went to the car and got out a Retriev-R-Trainer, put in the heaviest charge — purple. In spite of all his screams of foul, I "threw" a dummy 100 yards.

Bud Leavitt, outdoor editor of the *Bangor Daily News*, and Dick Warren, the paper's publisher, declared that I won the bet.

But the real winner is Arthur Johnson, inventor, mechanical genius, and ballistics expert. I contacted Arthur when I got the idea that there must be a better way than having an assistant throw dummies. Here we are about to throw a man to the moon, and retriever trainers were still using their arms. But the worst part for the nonprofessional trainer is getting an assistant, if he can't press his wife into service. Without a helper he just can't throw a dummy far enough.

It took a year for Art and me to work out the bugs.

Of course, this tool shouldn't completely replace the assistant. Not all the shots should be made off line. When an assistant is available, have him shoot it from off line. For field trials and hunting, the dog should learn to recognize where the guns are. There are many hunting situations where a dog is working for hunters in different blinds. He should learn to watch action around all blinds within his view.

1. **2.** **3.**

START TO PUT THINGS TOGETHER

There's no question what the dummy is. We started Jock off so young around the house that we had to make one puppy-sized to fit his mouth.

The noise of the gun isn't going to faze him, so we can put the two together with the new training tool the Dummy-Launch.

The whole point here is excitement and enthusiasm. Tease the pup; jump around swinging the dummy; feint a throw; do anything you can to make him want it like crazy. Spin around, talk it up, play like a ballet dancer, then slip the dummy on the spud of the Dummy-Launch and let it fly. Use a short blank; you want it to go only about 30 yards.

Let him go at will and don't insist on delivery to hand. Make it fun, make it easy. Don't make him have to hunt for it; let him see where it lands.

Don't overdo; quit when he's still anxious. The secret to hand delivery is plenty of affection. I've never had a dog yet that wouldn't deliver a dummy to hand from the beginning. Starting before he's twelve weeks old pays off in this department. He wants the dummy and he wants the fuss you make over him when he delivers all the way. If he doesn't deliver to hand, don't scold, but just don't make a fuss. Throw it again. Keep the whistle going when he's coming in. It will prevent him from dropping the dummy . . . delivery to hand is what we want.

It is extremely unusual in the retrieving breeds to have a young dog that shows absolutely no interest in retrieving by the time he's three or four months old. For the pup that just won't take to his game, find him a good home . . . fast. Force retrieving a retriever, as is sometimes necessary with the pointing dogs, is a painful procedure at best. (See *Gun Dog**)

* *Gun Dog* by R. A. Wolters. See page 100.

4.

5.

6.

Keep the excitement going, let him see the fall, keep it short.

THE NON-SLIP RETRIEVER

Work gets serious now. Make sure at this point the pup would rather retrieve than eat. Most trainers don't insist on steadiness until a dog is a year old. Jock, in these pictures, was as steady as a rock at just five months. Once the dog loves to retrieve, teaching him to be steady, as we teach it, won't dampen his enthusiasm to retrieve.

The technique for teaching steady is to hold the dog by the collar or the scruff of the neck. A dummy is thrown and the dog is restrained. This really doesn't dampen his enthusiasm. It seems only natural that he would assume that since you were holding him you didn't want him to retrieve. But, with all the excitement of this game, it takes only a short time for it to get through his noggin that it wasn't the retrieve that you *didn't* want, it was the SIT, STAY that you *did* want.

With the Dummy-Launch the job is make even simpler. Tie a stout rope or leash six or eight feet long around your body; snap it onto his choke collar.

STAY. STAY! STAY!!

Pictures on these and the next two pages show the setup. Here the dog broke to make the retrieve before he was commanded to do so. He inflicts his own punishment on himself. If he does wait to be sent, unsnap the leash and let him go. This is rare in a young pup.

Put the dog at HEEL, command SIT, STAY. Repeat the command STAY and shoot the gun. When he breaks for dummy set yourself for a shock. He doesn't know it yet but he's going to get one too...at the end of a rope. Jock only to go spinning twice and he learned. It was sure teaching; it took only five minutes and two jam-ups for him to decide it was best to wait until he was sent.

What about his enthusiasm to retrieve? Teaching not to break was learned so quickly that it didn't interfere with the fun of retrieving. There is no confusion on the dog's part as to what the trainer wants; you don't touch the dog. With the rope and the Dummy-Launch the dog still wants to retrieve, but he learns a positive thing...to depend on you, the trainer, to tell him when it's safe to go. Snap off the cord and let him at it.

Positive learning, cause and result, is a fast teacher. You can tell a kid to keep his hands away from the fire all you want, hold him back, too, but you'll never have to teach him again if he burns himself.

Most trainers don't like to teach steady too soon. But steadying a dog does *not* interfere with the enthusiasm to retrieve. You'll get better work from a steady dog because it's a well-known fact that a steady dog marks better than a breaking dog.

Just to make sure he has learned the lesson which he has inflicted upon himself, carry the long rope over your shoulder for a while. He won't know if it's attached or not.

DUMMY-LAUNCH...A EASY WAY

Take a chance. Command STAY. Shoot the dummy out. Don't make him wait long. If he should...

... break try to stop him with the whistle. Raise hell, put him back on the leash. But he waited, he didn't know if he was attached or not. Jam-ups taught him what he can expect.

THIS IS WHAT WE'RE AFTER...FEATHERS

The introduction to game is mighty easy. Retrievers have been bred for this. But there are some pitfalls.

When Tar was ten months old, Art Smith, outdoor editor of the *New York Herald Tribune*, and I went goose shooting in Maryland. Tar was well trained; he'd already won his first field trial, worked on pheasant, woodcock, pigeons, and duck. He could be handled to a blind retrieve. I only wish Art were as well trained in shooting as Tar was in retrieving.

I explained to Art that this was to be Tar's first goose and that it was important that the first bird be dead. A Canada is a big rough tough bird when wounded. It can raise hell with a young dog and scare the pants off him. As I finished my monologue, Art stood up and dropped a single that sneaked in from his side. It landed in the cornfield.

"Is it dead?" I asked.

"I shot it, didn't I?" he sneered, with an extra snarl on the "I."

Tar was sent. I glued my eyes on that goose. Tar streaked toward him. Six feet from the bird...the goose stood up to face his foe. Tar's momentum carried him in and he knocked the goose over. I held my breath. Tar and the goose went at it for a long time. Finally Tar moved toward us... backwards. He didn't know how to carry the heavy bird, so he finally decided to drag it back by the wing.

I took a deep breath and scoffed, "Great shot, Annie Oakley."

START 'EM ON BIRDS

Start with a freshly killed pigeon. Tease the dog with it and give it a short toss. (This need not be entirely new for him; I often play fetch with an eight- or nine-week puppy with a bird wing instead of a dummy.) In practically all cases that's it; the introduction is made and he loves it. And that may be your first problem. He will most likely get so excited that he'll get a little rough with it. Hold the bird in your hand so that if he goes to bite it he'll have to bite you first. Tell him to take it easy. When he settles down try him again.

Don't introduce him to the pigeons until he has learned to fetch the dummy. No use complicating the first lesson with the new smells. Don't be disturbed if he'll deliver a dummy all the way to hand but stops to play with the bird. The bird tastes so good that he just won't want to give it up. Don't scold him for this, but be firm and make him bring it all the way in.

This is where you may have to use the trick of calling him, whistling and running like hell away from him. But if he comes without the bird, reverse gears and attitude . . . scold him. Start over.

I always prepare a dog for the introduction to game by having him fetch a brush in the backyard. I confine this to the yard, hoping he won't get the idea that he's supposed to retrieve brushes. He'd look great some day following a cripple and coming back with someone's old discarded brush. The idea of the brush is to teach him not to clamp down on an object. The bristles will hurt.

Understand, too, that there isn't much nourishment in a dummy for a dog but a bird is another matter. When he does bring it in he has no natural desire to give his prize up. Your praise is going to have to please him more than a good meal would, so sing it loud and sweetly. If it's not enough he'll hang on like a drunk to a bottle. Then the tug of war starts. Have you ever eaten duckburger sprinkled with ground feathers? If you have it's your own fault. Don't pull a bird from a dog's stubborn mouth. *Push!* That's right, push it right down his bloody throat. If you try to see if his teeth are stronger than your hands, the duck is the loser. If you shove you'll gag him with it. He'll be pleased to spit it out.

A brush will teach soft mouth. If the problem gets serious, roll a pigeon in hardware cloth, let the sharp edges of wire stick out. He'll learn not to clamp down. A pup won't want to give up his prize. Besides pushing the bird down his throat, blowing into his nose will make him open his mouth.

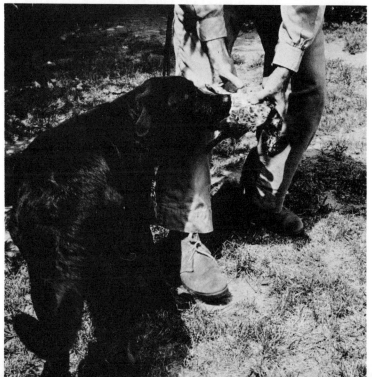

A break on his first live bird. We should've anticipated it. That's dog training for you.

BIRDS ON THE WING OR VICE VERSA

Roger, my son, who was taking this picture, was shaken as badly as I was when Jock broke for his first live pigeon. I didn't expect it, since he was under such perfect control with dummies. I should have known better and had someone out ready to pick up the bird . . . no waitie, no birdie.

But this is proof that you should start on dummies. Teach the commands first under the more controlled conditions of dummies. Since he does know what's expected, you'll be able to make the corrections easier. The added smell of live birds and the flapping of wings are so much added excitement for the dog that he forgets his manners. Just as the six-year-old boy seeing a platypus for the first time turns to his mother and says, "What in the *hell* is that!"

When he breaks during these first few lessons, he shouldn't be allowed to have the bird; but if there is nothing you can do about it as he goes give him the release command; at least he may learn that his going is associated with the signal. If he breaks after a few lessons, stop him with one whistle blast and give him a rousing what's for! If he's too excited for the whistle . . . back to the check cord.

SHACKLED DUCKS

The introduction to ducks is much the same as that for pigeons. Let him fetch a dead one on land, then in water. Correct him if he doesn't hold it properly. Some dogs like the butcher-shop hold — by the feet. Sit him in front of you. Open his mouth, put the body in his mouth and tell him nice things while holding it there. Incidentally, never let a dog romp with a bird.

Shackle birds by tying what amounts to their ankles, and tie the base of their wings together, too. Some use pipe cleaners for the job. That's O.K., but turn down the end of the wire. A stuck mouth can sure turn a pup away from live birds.

Shackled ducks will teach a dog how to handle a crippled bird. An unshackled cripple sometimes can do a lot of ranting and raving. A dog might react one of two ways. He might spook and swim home for protection, or he may charge in and settle the matter with one big chomp. Spooky and hard-mouth dogs are hard to correct.

Ducks are a retriever's real meat. The size, smell, and the splash add up to lots of excitement and can cause breaking trouble.

Lafe Page, a 130-pound hunter who guns off the rocks in Long Island Sound, had such a problem but now claims to hold the title for the most spectacular double ever made. After hearing how he killed his two ducks on two shots, I'm tempted to acknowledge his claim if his story is true.

Lafe and Puck, his massive 100-pound black Lab, were just beginning to understand each other when this story took place. Puck was great on dummies. Puck learned quickly that the boss shot the ducks and he was to swim out and bring them in. But Puck couldn't seem to understand why it was necessary to wait until he was commanded to go to do his job of retrieving. After all, no one was telling Lafe when to shoot the gun to do his job of killing the ducks; it didn't seem necessary to Puck that anyone need tell him when to do his job of retrieving. The boss had different ideas. He decided his headstrong black friend was going to learn to obey or be turned tail over teacups in the process. His plan was a good one. He tied a long rope around his own waist and attached the other end to Puck's choke collar. Now if he broke for the bird on shot he'd learn his lesson when he came to the end of his rope.

The plan was activated one cold November morning as they sat in the cover of their rock overlooking their decoys. A pair of blacks swung in for a look. Puck's ears stood up, so did Lafe. *Bang!* . . . a duck hit the water. Puck forgot his manners and charged forward. When he came to the end of his rope he just kept on going, dragging poor Lafe behind him. As Puck dug in across the shallow flats, Lafe, with upstretched arms, was frantically trying to zero in on that second duck. As Lafe hit the water with gun to cheek, the barrels crossed the path of the duck . . . he slapped the trigger and won his title.

This will teach us, no matter how good the dog is on dummies, be prepared for his first duck retrieve. To see what I mean, turn the page.

SHACKLED DUCKS...

WHAT FUN

A dog can be steady on dummies, pigeons, but ducks are a horse of another color. This is heart of the lettuce, this is the meat of the game. He has to learn that steady means STAY even if it's a hundred-dollar bill flying off.

Note setup. A rope is tied to the waist of the trainer. The other end is run through the ring of the choke collar and held in the hand. Show him the bird, throw it high in the air.

When it makes a big splash it'll most likely be too much for him. Off he'll go, he thinks. Hold him back, settle him. Make him sit. Then release him. Start over (center bottom picture).

Show five-month-old Jock the duck again. Blow once on the whistle, rousingly command STAY. Slightly jerk the check cord, just to remind him he's attached. Give the duck a good heave.

He's got the idea. If he weren't on the cord we would not make him wait too long. Now we hope the duck will quack to tantalize him more. Drop the cord, send him. Then praise him.

At about one year start teaching him to honor while another dog works. Start him on this rope device. He must learn to work only when it's his turn. When he's got the idea, in spite of his desire to go, ask permission of another handler with a trained dog so the other dog won't be upset if the young one forgets his manners and breaks. If he does, be ready with an upraised leash. Let him have it. Stop him by whistle, give him what for, hard.

1. Walk him at heel.

STOP...SIT ON SHOT

By this time I've assumed that you've shot some birds for your dog, and the Dummy-Launch has him completely prepared.

This lesson will do two things. It will be a rough steadying test for the dog. He'll soon learn that you want him to stay at your side until sent. If he breaks on the shot, just don't throw the bird for him. He'll soon get your drift. Start him over walking at heel. When he sits patiently after shot, throw the bird. If he breaks on throw, you've had it. Try to stop him. Bring him to heel. Then let him retrieve, but don't tell him he's good; in fact, don't tell him anything. Start over, talk a little rough to him, walk him at heel, shoot and go through it again. If the excitement of the gun and the flying bird is a bit much and he still breaks on the throw, put him back on the cord tied to your waist and slipped through his collar.

This is a rough breaking test and has fooled many a finished dog.

This lesson, sit to shot after the flush, also helps the hunter both for jump shooting and for upland hunting. It is a well-known fact that a breaking dog doesn't mark well. This may seem strange. Some hunters like to think that a dog gets a head start on the retrieve by busting in on shot. Not so with the retrievers. A sitting dog marks depth of fall better than a running dog.

While we're at it, let me mention that it's a good idea to keep rotating the classroom. Don't keep "selling your wares at the same old stand." A dog will learn to respond a certain way in specific surroundings. Take him to a new area and you'd think he was a complete idiot and doesn't understand what life's all about. This goes for all lessons, not just this particular one.

2. Shoot the gun.

3. If he doesn't break, throw the bird.

I've seen dogs get so excited on hearing the shot that they run helter-skelter like a chicken with his head cut off. They miss the fall. Gun noise often plays tricks. Sound can boom around and come from an opposite direction. A sitting dog has a better chance to recover, see the fall. What chance would a running dog have if a second bird was dropped elsewhere?

HEY WOODENHEAD...THAT'S NO DUCK

A decoy isn't for retrieving and it's easier and drier to teach it on land than water. The command to leave it alone is just that. LEAVE IT or a simple NO will accomplish the same thing. There isn't much to this lesson, but it will save you much embarrassment after the ducks come in. Another tip: when you're waiting for the ducks to come in, and the coffee is warming your gizzard, don't brag about your dog. I've seen it happen . . . wood!

Set the decoys out on the lawn and lead him through them. Command LEAVE IT if he wants to get familiar. Throw a dead duck among them. He'll ignore wooden blocks for a good bird.

THEY'RE FOR DUCKS
NOT DOGS

Some things you can't teach a dog; he's got to learn it himself. All you can do is to set up the situation and let him find out. We taught him on land to ignore the decoys; now he will have to learn to avoid them. Of course, we've helped him learn. We've strung the decoys together...some sneaky! Top picture, we throw a dummy out behind the blocks.

We send him and of course he goes straight...

...through toward the decoys, gets tangled.

Next time he's sent into the same setup, he avoids them like the plague. He goes around.

LET'S HAVE A LOOK AT THE DOG

We've put him through a lot for such a young dog, more than most trainers ever thought was possible. We interrupt the training here for a moment to straighten out some false thinking. Before this, some trainers have pushed a young dog along fast, but then something happened and they came to a wrong conclusion; they thought the early training was a mistake. On their second dog they waited. Here's what happened.

The dog was started and was doing rather well. All of a sudden the dog could do nothing right, and the trainer had the feeling the dog wanted to do nothing right. Just for argument's sake a point has to be clarified. We are referring to a dog that has been brought along as we have described so far, not one that has been pounded into the ground by harsh handling and overwork.

In the case of the dog as we have brought him along, we are developing his growing abilities. But even such a dog will revolt. Scientists have learned that every dog goes through this phase, no matter what the final product of training is going to be. It doesn't happen only in retrievers. This is one of the things that has fooled trainers about early learning. The word "phase" is a good one to describe it. The phase passes. But don't just wait for it to pass; this could interfere with his attitude toward learning. Think for a moment about kids. They go through the same thing. We now know with the dog that this attitude shows up like clockwork between the sixteenth and seventeenth weeks. It will happen again at about eight months, and you may see it again when he's just under two. Don't let it fool you; he's only expressing his independence, and will grow out of it quickly with a good attitude if you show him the way.

Training, when this phase develops, has to be handled differently for different dogs. In Tar's case he just refused to respond to commands. He tried to ignore training. He was easy to handle. I slowed down on my demands. Training periods were shortened. A whole lesson might have been cut to three minutes. But during those three minutes I saw to it that he did every damn thing I asked of him. In a week or so he saw that it wasn't going to work, and he again became a happy, cooperative pupil.

Jock, after being a retrieving fool from the time I first saw him in the kennel at five weeks, just stopped retrieving dummies at the exact age of fifteen weeks. I think he was one week precocious. This appeared practically overnight. Nothing out of the ordinary happened to him; he just decided to sniff around and then look at me as much as to say, "What are you standing there for? Go pick up the dummy yourself."

Well, the answer to that one was easy. If the pup wanted to play that kind of game with me, I could play it with him. I wait until a dog does a respectable job on dummies before I introduce him to pigeons (as explained before). But in this case the basic inborn desire to retrieve comes to the trainer's rescue. The pigeon was my secret training weapon. First day I held a bird in my hand. I let him smell it and I waved it around and feinted a throw. He got mighty interested. Back the bird went in his cage. The cage was left in sight for the first time. Next day, same thing with the added starter. I threw the bird. He streaked out. Stopped short, halfway. But the bird was too much for him. He ran in and retrieved. I tried a dummy . . . no soap. This was repeated for a week, but only one throw each day with the bird. By the time that week was up he would have retrieved my mother-in-law if I could have thrown her. He's been a retrieving fool ever since. This works wonders on a reluctant pup.

Every parent recognizes what I have just said. Don't consider this out-and-out defiance of authority. It's part of growing up. Don't lose your temper and show that you're more of a child than the dog. This experience in the long run, if handled with sense, will make the bond stronger between your dog and you.

SET HIM STRAIGHT

Every child gets rebellious and a dog goes through the same thing. Win your point and then quit for the day. Many trainers blow their stack, "lose" their dog at this crucial point.

If the youngster is too rambunctious for this, run some steam off him first. After a few...

HEEL AT THE CORRECT PLACE

With a young pup there is often a lot of fuss and bother training him to get to the correct place to start work. This little trick of leading him with the dummy seems to get the point across to him. After he gets the idea, this won't have to be used; he'll come into position of his own accord.

Don't forget, your dog is much lower than you are. Your eyes are almost six feet off the ground; his are only two feet. Make sure he can see what he's supposed to see over brush and terrain. If in doubt, get down to his level and have a look-see yourself.

If you're working with a couple of assistants, known as "guns," give the dog time to "find" them. When you're sure he has seen them, signal for one to throw the bird or dummy. If a shotgun isn't used, have the assistant holler a loud YHOO . . . YHOO to get the dog's attention. When the dog looks, the bird should be thrown. After the bird hits the ground, wait a second or so for the dog to fix its position; then signal for the second assistant to do his

... retrieves he'll be more cooperative. Lead him into position. When he's there blow SIT.

job in like manner. At first, of course, most of your work will be on singles. We won't move off them until he learns to pinpoint single falls. A few very simple doubles sprinkled in won't hurt. It's good for him to get the idea early that there might be more than one bird for him to fetch.

The Dummy-Launch reduces the need of assistants, always a problem for the amateur trainer. If you use this training device, you should still do some work using assistants. The dog's learning to locate the assistants or guns will be invaluable if you plan to field trial him. He'll then know the general area of the falls. The same thing goes for hunting. A dog often works for guns located in separate blinds.

If the dog freezes his gaze on only one gun, move him and sit him at heel facing the gun he missed. Don't try to turn his head with your hands.

If he still doesn't see, step forward with the leg next to him; cut off part of his view.

DON'T DROP...IT'S FOR THE TABLE

A dog should never drop a bird on a retrieve because the bird may be a cripple, and if dropped it just might fly off, leaving you with beans for supper.

It's only natural for a young dog to drop it at your feet. You'll have to teach him to deliver to hand, especially game. In his early lessons you'll have to play the part of a fast end. He'll come boiling back from the retrieve like a quarterback sneaking around the end. Intercept him on the fly. Take the bird from him on the run as he passes you. Praise him. After a while see if he'll hold the bird as he passes you and swings back to you. Finally, to break the dog of running past me at high speed, I stick out my foot and trip him. He gets the idea, and slows up and comes directly to heel.

If he drops, give him a lot of "what for." Don't lunge at him to try to get the bird or him. He's faster than you, but don't let him learn that. Never, but *never*, pick up a dropped bird yourself. If he learns that you will, he'll let you do it. Have him deliver to hand from the beginning. It's easier to teach now than later. If he absolutely refuses to hand deliver, run away. He'll most likely pick up the bird and chase after you. Then you can start over, take the bird from him. Here's the exception to the never-never rule. If he comes bounding after you without the bird, go back and pick it up and toss it a few yards. He'll pounce on it; now try to get him to hand deliver.

When he learns to hold, command SIT. A sitting dog, looking up at you, is not in a position to drop readily, and it shows good style.

A young dog will love to chew a bit on the bird, and you can't blame

Let me repeat. The going out is more instinctive than the coming in. We talk here about the pup who boils back with the bird. It's more likely that a young one will only come part way back. I've seen many a pup come almost to the handler, then decide to race back to the fall with the bird in his mouth to see if there was another one out there. Or he might be so proud that he races around to show everyone how wonderful he is. At this stage you'll see everything: the pup that brings it back halfway, then gets interested in something else, and the ones that boil back and at the last minute decide to play "Catch me" with you. You're not likely to have problems if you started retrieve early and often. If you do have them the only thing you can do is hack at him, stay with it. Never rush at him. The key to these pictures is the one above this copy. I hacked the dog into my feet. Then in the third picture I backed off. He started to get up. When up, I blasted once on the whistle. He obeyed and sat. I took the bird, gave him all the praise he wanted.

him. But discourage this; it leads to bad habits.

As a last resort, if he won't hold, open his mouth and put the bird in. Close your hand around his muzzle, command HOLD . . . HOLD. Don't be harsh on him in spite of the fact that you're not pleased. Give him time to learn.

SENDING THE DOG OFF

Everybody has their own ideas on sending or "giving a line" to their dogs. No one method is correct. I'll run through some of the different techniques, and you can decide which works best for you and your dog.

The most common command for releasing the dog, from a sitting position at heel, is his name. There's good thinking here. If the command were "fetch" for all dogs, all dogs in earshot might race for the bird, and the trainers would be left with ringside seats for a battle royal. Except, it doesn't exactly work that way, as you will see.

Some send the dog with the command BACK. It works. Still others combine the commands. When the fallen bird is a marked retrieve, the handler uses the dog's name to send him, and when the retrieve is a blind bird the handler uses the command BACK. This, too, makes sense. It signals the dog to the fact that he will now be handled.

Some handlers say nothing; some snap their fingers. I once saw a dog go on a sneeze.

As an experiment, I trained Tar a new way. Now I use this method, and think it best. I was much criticized for it by the field trial folk. But it worked like a dream. I send Tar from the line with two short, sharp blasts from the whistle. Right away some asked me what would happen if Tar was sitting and honoring and the other handler also used two blasts to send their dog . . . would Tar go? Answer, no. Just as two dogs trained to command BACK or two dogs with the same name won't break. I even gave someone my whistle to blow, for them to mimick my command. Tar still wouldn't go. In fact, the greatest fun I have when I demonstrate this is to set Tar up to be sent and blow only once. He won't go!

Since I'll be discussing this in connection with other commands later, I think it best to give an explanation here. It should be stated that you should decide for yourself after you read my theory whether you think it has merit. I'm not trying to convince others that their theory is wrong. All I can say is that I have trained with both methods, and the dog learned advanced handling faster and with less strain with the whistle method. Tar was an exceptional handler before he was a year old.

Incidentally, this method might be new for the retrievers, but sheepdogs have been trained along these lines for years . . . centuries.

It's this simple. All commands for *action* are to be whistle commands. The voice will seldom be used, but when it is used it will only be for reinforcement of the whistle or hand-signal commands.

When we started the pup we taught SIT by voice. Within a few days we change this to whistle . . . one blast. (See page 50.)

When we taught COME we taught it by voice and changed it to whistle . . . the continual rolling trill. (See page 64.) He responded to the whistle without the voice before he was out of kindergarten.

Let's look at this much of the picture, these first two commands. We're starting to talk about sending your dog for a retrieve. Flip ahead to page 116; you'll see that the dog is making a mistake that should be corrected. He didn't go where he was sent. To make this correction in a young dog you must have control over him. So, he makes a mistake. With one blast of the whistle you stop him. With the rolling trill you bring him in, start him over. This control makes training easier. Trainers ask why do I not stop him by voice and call him back by voice. The answer is simple. We're building our commands toward a dog that can be fully handled. Why train him when he's young to stop on voice when we'll require him to stop on whistle later? Why have him come in toward you by voice when he's young when he'll be required to do so later by whistle? These two whistle commands are the accepted methods now on finished dogs. So, we teach him one set of commands for his whole life, not change in midstream.

Next point. Where can you teach a dog his commands best? At your feet, where you can control him. Therefore, I sit my dog at heel with one blast. When I want him to come over and around to the position to sit at heel, I do it with the trill come-in whistle command. He may be required to come only ten feet, but at that short distance I can see to it that he does. This is the same procedure for a come-in command when he's 100 yards out in the field. Once he has this well learned, you can cut out using the whistle for heeling him up.

Next step. Releasing the dog for the retrieve, I give the appropriate hand signal, then I blast twice. *He does not move until I whistle twice.* This is the key to my system of fast learning of the handling commands OVER to the right . . . OVER to the left . . . BACK, by combining hand and whistle signals. This is the major difference of my system. *You will not allow the dog to move, even when he is sitting at some distance waiting for a direction command, until you are sure you know he knows which way he is supposed to go. He won't be released until you are sure it is toward the direction you are signaling.* This will all be explained and shown in pictures later. Now it is only necessary to give a fast rundown on the method so you will understand why I send the dog from line to make the retrieve with *two* whistle blasts. From this advantageous control position at my feet he learns not to move until released by whistle *no matter where he is.*

A young dog can handle early. Tar will never be a great field trial dog, but he won his first trial, a fun trial, in an All-Age gun-dog stake; he was the only dog of 23 to finish all tests: He had to be handled on the last bird. Age? Ten months! At 14 months he placed in a sanctioned Qualifying stake, and at 18 months he took a second place in a licensed trial Qualifying stake. At 17 months he took his first ribbon in a sanctioned Open stake. Qualifying and Open stakes require handling. But by age he was still only a Derby dog.

I thought out the whistle method one dreary day while sitting in a goose blind. We were two men to a blind, and the blinds were only 30 yards apart. But the weather was so bad we couldn't holler and be heard by the folks in the next blind. Only way I could get their attention was with the whistle.

Why have I expanded the whistle to all handling commands?

Once I tried the system, and this is important, I found the dog responded quicker and surer to the whistle than to the voice. The whistle is a real attention-getter for men, too.

Having to get someplace in a hurry in New York City, I hailed a cab by whistling through my teeth, a great asset in dog training. The cab driver jammed on his brakes and I got in. He said, "I usually never stop for people who whistle at me, I just keep going." He continued: "I don't like to be treated like a dog. The only reason I stopped," he explained, "was because of all those buttons on your hat. I wanted to know what they are."

I took off my hat, threw it up to him, saying, "They're all field trial buttons." He said, "What do you do?" and I answered, "Train dogs." He slumped over the wheel.

In the pictures I demonstrate how I send the dog by arm signal. First make sure the dog is lined up in the direction you want him to go. He won't run around corners. His first movement will be in the same direction his spine is pointing. Note where I place my hand. Some trainers place the hand over the head. Some out in front. Some to the side of his head. In all cases, the arm is parallel to the dog's body, and the dog's body is pointed like an arrow to the target. You and your dog can decide the best placement of the hand.

On a single retrieve, why is it necessary to give a young dog a line? Well, it's not. He saw it fly. He hasn't taken his eye off it, and could run to it just as well with or without the line signal with your hand. But, once again, this is training now for the future. You're hoping somewhere along the road that through repetition he'll start to put together the facts that the bird is out there and that that big fat hand sitting next to his eye is pointing to the same place. Later, on a blind, he's not going to know where the bird is, so we're hoping he'll take the cue and take a line.

SENDING THE DOG OFF

Be sure the dog's spine is in line with the direction you're going to send him. Get the directing hand out where he can see it. Even if the bird is in plain sight and only ten feet in front of him give him the direction. On a close bird he'll learn to realize that the hand is his guide...we hope. Your motion for sending him is like a bowler releasing the ball. It's a graceful step forward. The command to go is given as you move.

LIKE THE MAIL...DELIVER UNDER ALL CONDITIONS

The pup's been given rather simple retrieves up to this point. They should continue to be simple, but conditions should change. For picture purposes this body of water is small but it will demonstrate the idea. The next three spreads of pictures will show how to lengthen and to vary the dog's retrieve. Take him step by step. Teach him young that obstacles are fun to surmount. Get him out on islands; get him to cross islands. Teach him to leave points of land and to go onto points. Single retrieves are best where the conditions are new and different.

1. The dog is about four months and is ready to enter the big world. The first retrieve...

2. ...is baby stuff. You're at water's edge and he's sent just off the bank and returns.

3. Now we start to build. We throw to the other bank, not just in the open water. We've...

4. ...increased the distance of the swim. This all looks simple, but we're putting a...

5. ...lot of simple things together. Build on simple tests for the pup. (Turn the page.)

BY LAND OR SEA

A young dog will often swim to the far shore and when he gets there forget his mark. If he gets to the other side and just runs the bank, call him back. Leave the dummy there and throw another one. All the water retrieves he has made so far he's picked the bird up in the water. I know it sounds simple, but actually he has to learn to climb the bank and, like Columbus, discover land. These first retrieves across water and onto land should be in low cover. The first time Jock crossed water, then land, and came to more

6. It's land, water, then land . . .

7. . . . From water to land, a new experience.

water, he stood up on his hind legs, swung a look back at me as much as to say, "Look what I found!" Then he dived in.

Gradually increase the distances on both sides of the water. If he starts to drop the bird after he comes back through the water, give him a good scolding. Go back; set up the tests again where you are close to the water. Get the bird from him before he drops it. Only praise him on full hand deliveries from now on.

8. We move the dog back and throw dummy deeper. Now it's farther by land on both sides...

...and a swim in between. We're building memory and negotiating obstacles. (Turn the page.)

TRY ALL THE ANGLES

When you were young you learned all the angles; same goes for the dog. The pictures show him learning in water, but on land they're just as important. A dog running along a slope tends to run downhill. A ditch, a path or road will tend to throw a dog off mark, especially if he approaches it from an angle. Abrupt change of cover from a mowed field to a cornfield will cause his compass to swing. Take all these situations as they come up as new problems. Make the retrieves short and at all the angles. When he charges straight toward the dummy without regard for terrain, start to lengthen the retrieve

As he learns one lesson, take him on to the next. These last three pictures of the set add two new problems: heavier cover and sending him on an angle. To start, the angle should be about 45 degrees. You should send him first from water's edge when starting angles. This will help teach him to go directly into the water and not run the bank. Gradually move back. Turn page, see what can go wrong and how whistle obedience can save you.

by throwing the dummy farther and moving back so that he has to cover more land before he reaches the "barrier." When you send him on these angle retrieves, be sure to make much of setting him up on line. Be sure his spine points correctly. Even more important, overemphasize the sending arm signal. Let him wait a little longer on line ready to go. We're trying to convince him that the sending arm is pointing to that bird. Follow the arm. It'll lead to the bird no matter what the angle or the terrain. How many times I wish I could say to him and have him understand, "Look, stupid, what do you think I'm doing with my arm, waving it in the breeze to keep it cool?"

Field-trial folks have always been critical that my dogs respond to whistle commands so...

...early. Here's a situation, an angle throw. He runs the bank to cross the bridge. Makes...

...sense, but not what we want. The whistle stops him, brings him back. We teach him...

WE ALL MAKE MISTAKES...

But let's nip them in the bud. Being obedient to hand directions and whistle commands at only a few months of age is important so that necessary corrections can be made before bad habits are formed. It's so much easier to learn to do it right now than relearn later.

When he responds to the COME-IN whistle don't scold him for making a mistake on the retrieve. Say nothing; start him over. Being called off a retrieve is a form of reprimand itself. You don't want him to learn that the COME-IN whistle means a scolding. But he must learn to do things as you want him to do them, not as he wants. Make him do it over and over until he gets your drift. Then make a big fuss.

Some trainers shoot an air pistol at the dog's rear end as he breaks or takes a wrong line. I've *never* had to do this. You won't either. If Tar starts wrong, I just whistle, he'll stop and sheepishly come back to heel and await the recast or resend.

Of course, once a dog is older and he pulls these tricks . . . shake him up! Air guns and electric shock sticks are just not necessary. They may be fine if you're training ten dogs, where time is essential.

...that's not what we want. Follow my sending hand signal. Go by water. If I could not stop him, how could I correct him?

EXTEND THE RETRIEVE

By this time your retriever will have gotten the idea that he's a retriever. If you're not sure, or better yet if he's not sure, don't advance him to this lesson until he is sure. We want him to bound out for the retrieve; then is the time to extend him.

A path through a field is the best place, or a dirt road will do. We're not trying to fool the dog in these retrieves. We're showing him where the dummies are dropped. We want him to get used to the idea of going long distances to make the pickup.

Start this game at short distances and gradually work up to 150 yards or more. He'll get the idea very quickly, but don't stop when you're sure he's learned this. From time to time go back and play it over.

Let him see that we're dropping them. We're not trying to fool him. Walk him on down the path. Send him for the first one (top right picture). Send him back again. Tar was so young in the picture that we were still using the small puppy dummies. He learned fast.

Photographing a black dog in heavy cover is not easy. Look close and you'll see what he's up to. Sticking with it, searching out the fallen game will pay off in dividends on a hunting trip. We threw a scented dummy — a bird would have been better — into heavy cover and sent him in. After a good fight in the brush he came out to find out what we expected of him in that stuff (upper right). We told him in no uncertain words what was expected. So he scampered back in to see what he could find (lower left). He finally came out, dummy on one end, wagging tail on the other. A happy ending for all (lower right).

HUNT IN HEAVY COVER...

And don't come home without the bacon. It's a good idea to scent the dummies with a few drops of anise extract or one of the prepared bird scents. Better yet, use live birds for this lesson. You'll be teaching him two things: that you're going to be damn unhappy if he decides to quit without finding the bird, and to use his nose for hunting. Make sure there's some wind stirring. Throw the dummy into the wind. Send him so he'll run into the scent.

Under ideal conditions a dog will scent a bird up to twenty-five or more yards, but since you don't have such a good nose you really can't tell how the conditions are. Some weeds, such as catnip, give odors that are very confusing to a dog, so have patience with him.

When the dog learns to use his nose and stays out there hunting until he finds what he's after, then you can start using the wind from all quarters. Conditions are rough on the dog when the wind blows in the same direction that he's running. Crosswinds aren't too tough.

Set up all kinds of tests using the wind, terrain and cover.

REMEMBER THE MARK

When we started the pup retrieving we never made him wait at heel before he was sent to the fall. It's always good to release a pup that is starting just as the bird hits the ground. Often a young dog that is held too long on line will look up to the trainer, waiting for the release command. Taking his eyes off the mark can really mix up a youngster.

Now, with more experience under his belt, deliberately make him wait. We're trying to make him orient the fall with the landscape and develop his depth perception.

This spread of pictures and the next two spreads are good lessons to develop good marking ability. Also, how well trainers know that a dog can lose the ability of pinpoint marking once he has it. They seem to go through phases. So take such a dog that seems to have forgotten all he ever knew, and try some of these tests. Threatening him with being turned into a rug won't help this matter. Waiting on line to make a simple single retrieve will bring a dog back.

Shoot the dummy.

"You mark, I'll smoke."

Incidentally, if a dog can't seem to make a retrieve don't let him just roam all over the countryside. After a sensible period go out and pick the bird up yourself or have an assistant do it. But I never let the dog have the bird under these circumstances. Most trainers do. They throw the bird up and make a noise to get the dog's attention. Of course nuthead runs over, picks up the bird and runs hell-bent-for-election back to you as happy as a lark. As far as I can see, he hasn't learned much.

It's better to call him as you pick up the bird. Let him see where it was and that you have it. Teach him, we want him to pinpoint the fall or he gets no bird. Walk back to the line. Say nothing to him, except possibly, "Stupid," under your breath a few times. He'll walk back to the line with his tail mighty low. Then in a pleasant tone of voice say such things as: "Come on, boy. We can do better than that. Let's try again." He'll get the change of tone, and perk up. Start the test over. When he gets the dummy this time, stop and make a real fuss over him.

"Remember the mark?"   **"Let's see."**

123

Shoot a dummy. Change position. He looks back while walking. We'll see if he has it marked. Jock is only nine months old here. Heeling him off line takes control. But he's up to it.

LET'S MOVE AND REMEMBER IT

Set the dog up and let a dummy fly. Let him get a good look at it. HEEL the dog and move back before sending him off. Now he has to remember more than the depth of the fall; he's got to remember where it fell in relation to the terrain. After he has learned this one, try him on memory falls. Have the bird or dummy thrown so that he sees it only in flight for a short period of time. It's good to start memory falls so that the flight is high and the bird falls in water. He won't see the splash because of the terrain that blocks his view, but he will hear the splash. Once he does these, try them on land.

FOR THE NUDNIK AND THE HUNTER

Some dogs retrogress. This is natural, as we have said before. When the dog gets into this state, try a duck that has only his wings shackled. Hold the dog on line and let the duck walk off. This will teach him to mark. This will also help a dog that hunts short. He'll sit there on line with eyes glued on that duck as it walks off in the low cover. You can let that duck walk a hundred yards, and when he's released he'll nail that bird.

This lesson is excellent for training the dog to follow and hunt out a crippled bird. Let the wing-shackled duck walk into heavy cover and hide. Then send the dog. He'll learn to use his nose. Learning to trail by scent can put a lot of meat on your table.

Show him the duck and let his mouth water. Release it and command him to stay at heel. For picture purposes we did not let the duck waddle off too far. The dog will watch every move of the fowl. He'll mark with precision. This good training trick develops marking.

These pictures demonstrate how to start on doubles. Use low cover so he can see. You want him to get the idea that there is a second bird out there to fetch. Make the angle of the two dummies wide so he won't be confused about the second retrieve. Note how we take our time, in the third picture down on the next page, to set him up in the correct direction.

DOUBLES, ANYONE?

I'm sure you've already tried your dog on doubles while he was still studying singles, but now we should take it up in earnest. Take him back to that lawn. We want him to see everything. The lesson we have to teach him is that there's another bird out there after he comes back and delivers the first.

Now set him up. Send off two dummies. Make the second bird you throw the longer of the two. A dog 99 out of 100 times will run first for the last bird down. Make these doubles widespread. You don't want him to get the idea to go back in the same direction on the second retrieve as the first. Make sure he can see the second dummy when you're about to send him for it. That's the reason for using very short cover.

Keep him doing these retrieves. You'll know if he's getting the idea of this game if, on the way in to you with the first bird, he shoots a glance over to the next bird he's to retrieve. Also, when you heel him to send him off for the second dummy, if he knows what he's about he'll line himself up in the correct direction. If not, be sure you do it for him.

Within a week of this you'll be able to reduce the angle of the two dummies. Finally you'll have him doing short over and unders. That is, two birds in a straight line, one farther out than the other. He'll take the short one first, then go back in the same direction for the other one. This isn't easy for him to do. Start him out with the long bird being shot last. If he picks it up first, he won't have to go so far for the second. Then reverse the order.

Send him for a dummy. As he comes in throw one toward him. Start the COME IN whistle...

DON'T SWITCH

This is the time to teach him that he's to do one thing at a time. The bird in his mouth is just as good as the one that's still out there to be retrieved. While he has been making the simple retrieves up to this time, you should have been hitting the whistle with the COME-IN command as soon as he makes the pickup. Then bring him all the way in "on the whistle." Now we'll tempt him with a second throw when he's coming back. It's a short-enough distance so that if he goes to drop the one bird to pick up the other, you're close enough to run out and make the correction. Sound like a fishwife if you want to. Scare hell out of him. Let him see that you don't like that sort of thing.

On a double, after he makes the pickup, if he starts to run toward the other fall, stop him by whistle and bellow NO . . . NO and start the COME-IN whistle. Take a few running steps towards him as you do this. Make him think at least that you could catch him if he doesn't obey.

For the dog that doesn't seem to get the point, make the double retrieve

...he'll stop and look. Work the whistle and praise him. Switching birds loses hunting time.

one water and one land. Now he won't switch. When he does this right, make a big fuss over him.

It's about time now that you broke him in on pheasants. The smells are great! The way you do this is the same as introduction to pigeons. Use as many as your pocketbook can stand. The more live birds your dog can get, the better for him. Live birds cause an excitement that dummies never duplicate. Young dogs may tend to switch on live game, so now is the time to nip this in the bud. We want to teach him to cover the ground directly to and from the fall with as little disturbance as possible to the cover. We don't want a dog horsing around out in the field. We don't want him flushing game by error or flaring ducks about to set into the stool.

EXTEND HIS KNOWLEDGE

A dog brought along at the top of his ability should be able to do simple land triples and water doubles and triples by the time he's a year old. We start him off on triples in a mowed field, again where he can see. Then take him to low cover where he has to use his nose and eyes to hunt. Finally it's done in heavier cover, at least with one of the birds of the series. It's not good to start either the doubles or triples on all heavy cover. Mix them up with land and water. Lengthen one or more out to 150 yards. Shoot a bird that falls right in front of him as a breaking test; add this to a long single. This short diversion bird can mess up many a good dog. The point here is to mix them up. Use the wind, the cover, the terrain. When he goofs, run the same test over until he gets what you're after. Then when you think he has all this, take him back to the real simple retrieves. Remember, the biggest mistake most trainers make is thinking that because he has learned XYZ the dog knows his ABC's. Take him back to the ABC's; it'll pay off.

HANDLING, THE MIRACLE OF THE RETRIEVERS

The most spectacular job of the retriever is handling. A dog that handles well looks great and so does his handler. As we have mentioned before, this is a must for the waterfowl hunter's dog. But spectacular things aren't necessarily the most difficult to learn. There are some tricks here, and it's really easy to teach this to an eager dog.

The most important thing — and I might as well mention it right at the beginning — is the dog's undivided attention. There's only one way to get it. The dog must sit on one blast of the whistle, face you and wait for directions. If a dog is running around hunting and you blow one blast for SIT and he doesn't, but gives you only a fleeting glance as you give him the direction signal, you might as well spend your time waving at girls going by in fast cars. Your result will be the same. Let me repeat this important point: Don't try to teach handling until you can get his undivided attention on the SIT whistle at any distance. But now we have taught this from a very early age. Our pups sat on whistle at twelve weeks. By the time he was six months old, this command was firmly set in his gray matter. We started the whistle instead of the voice at the early age for this very purpose. Now we can put it to use.

The next important point is that the dog must learn to believe in you. You'll do this by incentive training. He'll learn that if he follows your command, you'll lead him to the bird. Now, if you were going to train a circus dog you'd do the same thing. But the reward would be a tidbit. The tidbit for the retriever is the retrieve. We'll teach him to take a line and to follow hand signals by making him learn that we'll help him find the bird.

Now we have two things: the dog's undivided attention, cooperation or teamwork. The next thing is to teach him what the hand signals are. That we will show. It's easy if we start early.

The next point: we will not release the dog from the SIT attention position until we, the handler, know that he'll go in the desired direction.

The last step is to extend all this to cover large areas of ground and water.

There are two things to remember. In teaching handling, don't work for long blinds. Keep them short. Let the dog be successful. Leave distance for the future. Wait until he's sure of his job. If he does get confused, don't keep blasting at him. Stop and start over. Shorten the distance. The other important thing is to make sure the dog realizes that he's being controlled or handled. When the dog receives his first whistle to sit, that's the end of his hunting on his own. If that dog takes a wrong turn, hit him with the whistle fast. Sit him down and give him the correct hand signal. Unfortunately, in field trials the fewer whistles a dog must be given to get the blind bird, the better the job. Luck, terrain, wind, and so on, have much to do with the job. It's more important that the dog doesn't refuse the whistle or the handler's direction signal, no matter how many whistles you have to give him.

If you let him hunt hoping he'll stumble on the bird, you'll have a hard time teaching the dog to take his cast OVER or BACK for any distance in a straight line.

It's best to teach all this on land. If he just doesn't understand, or if he just decides that he's not going to play your game, it's rather hard to get him to make the correction if he's swimming around in some pond.

You'll also find that you can have him do anything you want if he's working rather close in to you. But he may take the attitude, when he's a hundred yards out . . . the hell with you. Put on your track shoes and get out and teach him a thing or two. Keep the working distance short; he'll work better and you won't get a heart attack.

So often new trainers say that they could never teach a dog to handle. Nonsense. It's a step-by-step logical procedure. We take the sting out of these lessons by starting the dog early . . . way before he's a year old we prepare him for handling.

When do I start all this? Well, it shocks most trainers, but Tar, as you remember, sat on whistle from the time he was eleven weeks old. He understood hand signals as a backyard game at the tender age of sixteen weeks. It works.

LET'S START...BUT WAIT

Here's the way to start the handling. This game is started as only single retrieves; doubles and triples will be added later. Set up the triangle situation as in the pictures. Whistle SIT. Show him the hand signal for stay. Command STAY. Throw the dummy. If he breaks, try to stop him with the whistle. If he won't stop, have the assistant pick up the dummy before he can get to it. He'll soon learn to wait or he won't get the dummy.

Teaching him at this tender age that he isn't to go until released is important. He has to be just as steady out in the field as he is at your side.

The four pictures on this page show the setup and what has gone wrong. He was commanded to stay but he broke before he was told to go. His reward for breaking? The assistant got the dummy ahead of him. Jock was only a few months old when he started this new game...

...but he learned fast, as the four pictures on the next page show. If he waited for the command to go and its supporting hand signal, he got his just reward, the dummy and praise.

134

FOLLOW ORDERS...THE REWARD

Sit him down again. Throw the dummy at the assistant's feet. If he waits, give him the hand signal. He'll get so excited to go that he may turn and sit facing the dummy. Now you know he'll go in that direction. Release him with the two blasts of the whistle. He learns what the arm signal means and the two blasts or command OVER means go.

Repeat this procedure for an OVER to the other side. When he can do these two, have the assistant move to "second base." Throw the dummy over his head. Give the BACK hand signal. Send him off.

BASEBALL IN THE BACKYARD (PICTURES, NEXT PAGE)

This is backyard baseball. He sits in the pitcher's box, but the trainer pitches and he catches. Here's the way you set up the game. Take him to the center of the yard. Command SIT, STAY. You walk to home plate and pitch the dummies to first, second and third base, but in any order you want. He sits and stays. Blast once on the whistle for attention. Start off by giving the arm signal for the last dummy that was thrown. His attention, of course, was last on this one. Command him to go. I use two blasts on the whistle as a release. Most trainers call OVER for side casts or BACK for the cast behind

Here is the setup for baseball. Sit the dog down at the pitcher's box. You walk to home plate. Command STAY. Take three dummies. Throw one to the right, one to the left, and one over his head. He's learned from the earlier game not to break while you make the setup.

him. But as you will see later, I also send him from this position with a double command. The two blasts he learns first. As he goes I immediately call BACK or OVER. Now he'll learn both commands, and I can use the voice command as a reinforcing command if needed, as you will see.

When he brings in the correct dummy, line him up to take the next one of your choice and send him for it from heel. But watch your dog; if he lines up to take the one at first base and you wanted the one at second, line him up for the one he wants, and send him.

Let him make a home run and clean up the last base. Set him up again and start over. After he gets the idea, *don't* send him for the last dummy thrown. Send him for one of the other two. Now he gets the idea what the pointing arm means. If he starts to make a mistake, stop him with one blast. Go out and sit him down in the pitcher's box. Go home and start over.

We'll show later how to extend the game in the field. But for the field trialer who doesn't want his dog to get used to handling until he's out of Derby, this game should be played only in the backyard. He'll have learned the basic commands for handling at four or five months, but won't know to depend on the handler for these commands out in field conditions.

BASEBALL IN
THE BACKYARD

Remember a dog goes for the last bird down. Here, the one over his head was last so it's where you start. You must have his undivided attention. Show him the BACK hand signal, arm straight up. Blast twice on the whistle which is the MOVE command. Move your hand in a forward motion and off he goes. Retrieve the other two dummies from the heel position.

Set the game up again. Make the last dummy down the left side as shown. Send him with whistle and hand signal. The left arm is now used. Point first, then bend the elbow and throw the hand out in the direction he's to move in. Do the same thing to the right after you make this setup, right dummy last down. After he gets this idea, do not send him for the last bird down. Send him for one of the other two. But the trick here is to keep him seated in the pitcher's box until you're sure he will go in the correct direction. How can you tell? He'll look or glance that way. If you are still not sure, jerk your body and give a slight motion in the direction of the correct dummy. If he reacts and moves slightly that way, send him by whistle. If not, take a step or so in that direction. He'll get you. If you have trouble teach OVER casts first. Tar could play the game with precision when he was six months old. He started at 16 weeks.

Blast once, SIT. Get his undivided attention. Give the hand signal. Wait for his response. Don't wait for him to look back. Blast twice. He'll cast in the direction he's looking...

HERE'S WHAT WE'RE AFTER

We're going to show you here what the final product will be. It's easier to understand all the next steps in teaching handling if you know what we're trying to achieve. Of course, it's O.K. for me to jump ahead to explain it to

... Same thing in the other direction. Let me repeat. To get results in handling, he has to be seated and looking at you waiting for directions. A dog that won't stop won't handle.

you, but don't you try to do this to the dog.

The preliminary pictures we haven't shown here are the dog sitting at HEEL, the SEND-OFF command, two whistle blasts or voice BACK. The dog lines out following your arm direction. When he's out far enough give the one whistle blast to stop. He turns, faces you and waits for the direction command.

Three dummies have been hidden out of sight. One to his left, one to the right and one back behind him. He has just looked at us on the one blast. We gave him the arm signal for the direction that we'll want him to go. That's where we take up these pictures.

He knows to wait. He will not be released until we tell him to go. He therefore sits and looks to see if he can see the dummy in the direction that we have indicated. This is our signal that *he'll go in that direction*. When we're convinced, we released him with the whistle . . . two blasts. As he gets up to go, the whistle will often attract his attention and he may glance our way. That's why I like to put a lot of body English in giving these arm signals; just like the pool player who twists all over the place after the ball has been hit. He "helps" the ball into the right pocket.

Remember when I mentioned that some people send their dog from line by his name for a marked retrieve and by the command BACK for a blind retrieve? It gave the dog a signal as to what was going to be expected. It's a similar situation in this case. If it's a short cast OVER or BACK, I use only the whistle. But if it will be a long cast OVER or BACK after he's been released from his waiting position, I add the OVER or BACK voice command. This is to signal him that I want him to go a long distance on this cast.

This method has degrees of control. I mentioned before that the whistle is a sharper command, and the dog responds to it better than the voice, and the whistle carries farther than the voice. Of course, after he learns all this, you'll find that he'll handle on either voice or whistle alone. A dog soon learns what you want. He may even get so perceptive after a while that a slight movement in the right direction on your part will signal to him what you want.

As a boy I had a dog that I trained at the same time I learned to look cross-eyed . . . a great sport for a boy. One day I told the dog to sit. He refused. I raised my voice and my hand and for some reason crossed my eyes. From then on, all I had to do to make him obey was to cross my eyes.

This is not recommended for retriever training, except for personal therapy for the trainer.

BACK command is handled the same as the casts to the side. I use the whistle to send him, but reinforce it with the voice BACK or OVER commands when I want him to take this cast for a long distance. This really gives me an extra control in handling the dog.

The next 20 pages have to do with taking a line, the first step in handling. You have to get your dog out there in the right direction. A straight line is fastest. Here's the start.

HOW TO SUCCEED...I BELIEVE IN YOU

Tar is only six months old, but already he believes in me. Hide an assistant with a dummy. Send the dog from heel. Release him with the command and have him take your line. If he won't do it and goes off like a drunken sailor, the assistant won't throw the dummy. But if he takes your line when he passes the assistant, have him heave the dummy ahead of the dog. The dog won't know where it came from, but it will be like manna from heaven. Move the assistant around so the dog won't get wise to him. Do this in different areas so he'll get the idea that this "good news" always happens. Set up the test in water. Remember, he's very young; this is only the start so make these very short retrieves. Twenty-five yards is plenty. Later we'll extend him.

Once we've this much accomplished, and believing in you is a great deal, we must teach him to take the line, and the line by definition is straight. He'll have a desire to do it his way, and that may be "direct" by way of the corner saloon.

Turn the page and see how we teach him to go through obstacles, not around them.

143

DON'T GO ROUND THE MULBERRY BUSH

1.

2.

3.

4.

5.

6.

At first it's hard to get through his big black head the fact that a line is straight, not curved, round, or zigzag. In these pictures we try to show him a line is straight, even if it has a dip in it. No. 1, we throw a dummy across a ditch. We're only standing a few yards back from the lip of the ditch. We send him in No. 2, he goes through the ditch and retrieves in No. 3. No. 4, we do the same thing, but go back 20 yards from the hole. No. 5, he was sent in a line but saw an easier way, around the mulberry bush and the ditch. "No you don't!" we holler and stop him by whistle. Bring him back and send him, and stop him and start over until he goes the way we want him to. Straight, as in No. 6.

RUN ON THE BANK...GET NO CASH

Young dogs have a tendency to run the bank. I don't see this as a major fault if it's the fastest way to the bird. It's objected to in field trials; they want to see a dog go direct.

You can release a dog from line by whistle only, without the hand directional signal, but if the direction signal is given he should follow it. If this becomes a problem and he doesn't take your line but goes his own way, work him from the edge of the water. Each time you send him, step back. He'll gradually get the idea to go straight in. If he goofs, take him back to the water's edge and start over. When he learns not to run the bank, after he's been sent for a retrieve, you walk down to the edge of the water. When he comes back with the bird, this may prevent him from running the bank coming home.

Don't try to send a young dog on angles into the water. This will tend to make him run the bank.

1.

2.

3.

It's true that running the bank in a hunting situation may enable the dog to make the retrieve faster. But if you send him from heel by giving a direction with your hand and he veers off to run the bank, he's just telling you to go to hell and is going to do it his way. A run-the-bank situation such as this one is another means to hammer away at him that the line must be followed. After all, we're trying to build toward the blind retrieve. He's not going to know where the bird has fallen. He must depend on you, so if he bank runs instead of hitting the water, he may be going opposite to where the bird fell. Stop him by whistle (top picture). Call him in. Resend him. When he goes by water, you walk down to the water's edge so that when you whistle him back with the bird, he may come by water. It may look closer to him. I'm not too sure how important straight-line return is — it looks mighty impressive to see.

TEACHING LINE...A WRONG WAY

The picture on the left looks good but it's a bad practice. We had the dog sitting on line; we gave him the release signal and the arm directional signal to go. When he moved out in front a good distance, we threw a dummy ahead of him. This is to teach him that if he takes a line in the direction of the arm signal he'll get his reward, the "surprise" dummy. It's O.K. to start a dog with this method, but note the pictures below. In very short order the dummy is no longer a surprise. He soon learns that you really had it behind your back all the time. Note how Tar turns his head, anticipating my throw. This will encourage a dog to pop. If you want to test out what I mean, after you do this a few times don't throw the dummy. He'll go out about the distance of your throwing arm, turn and wait for the throw.

If you do start with this method, watch your dog. If he catches on to you, stop doing it. The hidden assistant shown earlier is a much better system.

On most of the simple retrieves so far, your dog won't really need the arm directional signal that we've been giving him. But again, the reason we've been doing it on these marked retrieves is to put across to him that the arm that points his way always points to where the bird is. When the time comes and the retrieve is blind, and he won't know where the bird is, we're hoping that he'll remember that in the past the arm always pointed a straight line to the bird.

The camera catches the dog anticipating the throw. It can lead to a serious fault, popping. If he does develop this popping habit when being sent for a blind, do something about it fast. When he turns around as much as to say, "What do you want now, boss?" charge at him with flailing arms, holler, "GO ON! GO ON!" You aren't pleased, let him really know about it.

TEACHING LINE...NEXT STEP

This time there are no dummies up the sleeve. We're not trying to fool the dog. Blind retrieves are a long way off. The picture on the left shows the setup. A dozen or more dummies are put out on a flat lawn. We all know where they are. So, like the second grader that he is, we have him do his ABC's over and over a dozen times. Now we're trying to get through that big black head that the directional sending arm always points to the dummies.

He'll learn this game very quickly. Keep changing the starting point. Make the distances he has to go longer and shorter.

Once he's learned this, we'll go on to the next step. But go back over this even after he's advanced beyond it.

We sent him up and back 16 times. He got tired, but we hope he noted where the arm pointed.

A STRAIGHT LINE...BY TRIANGLE

Now we want him to learn to become more dependent on the sending arm. In the last game he was always sent back to the same place. He knew the place because there was a pile of dummies there. Now the conditions change for each retrieve. That is, we start him from a new place for each retrieve, and he makes the pickup in a different area each time. The only thing that's constant is the direction pointed out by that sending arm. *It always points toward the bird.*

1.

2.

This triangle game looks complicated, but it's not. We show it here in low cover so you can see how the game is played. It should be played in cover so the dog can't see the dummies. No. 1, throw a dummy, send the dog. No. 2, when he goes out, drop a dummy behind you. Leave it. No. 3, walk out one arm of the triangle. Throw a dummy. He's retrieving it in this picture. You have dropped one behind you once again. No. 4, walk to the last point of the triangle. Drop a dummy behind you. There is a photo mistake here. The right-hand dummy is there, but it was not included in the picture. Now the triangle is formed. Send the dog for the first one that was dropped. No. 5, the dog comes down to retrieve that first one. When he returns to you, walk him down to this first position. Send him for the dummy off to the right. Walk him out to spot he just retrieved from. Send him in the last direction for clean-up. If you want to go around again, drop off the dummies at each spot. Gradually make the size of the triangle bigger. This is where the Dummy-Launch comes in handy.

3.

4.

5.

153

NOW WE GO AROUND THE CLOCK

Take a dozen dummies and send them out to every point on the clock. Throw some short and throw long ones with the Retriev-R-Trainer.

Then at random pick the one you want. Face him toward it and send him. Now he's getting the idea of the game. The hand points the way.

MOWED "H" ... GRADUATE WORK

The best place to teach handling is in a mowed path. I use the word "in" because the low mowing surrounded by the high cover will confine the dog's direction.

Take a big field and mow it in the shape of an H. For picture purposes here we used only one-half of the long arms of the H; you can get some idea how big a field is needed. Each arm was over 200 yards long. The crossbar of the H was about 30 yards wide.

This is the classroom for Tar. Any dog who has been brought along steadily in his work will be ready to accept this training at about twelve to fifteen months of age.

The first thing we do is to get him used to the idea of using the paths. This will be a good means of extending him out as far as the full 200 yards.

Turn the page and you'll see the next step, the mowed path blind.

1.

This might look like we're regressing, but we aren't. We're extending him quite far. As a by-product of this game, we're teaching him overs and unders. Many times it is confusing for a dog to run back over the land for a second bird. I've seen them stop, you can almost see them think: "I've been over this ground, where the hell is that second one?" In the pictures we sit him, spread out the dummies, and send him out for them. He's ready for controlled blinds on the path.

2.

3.

4.

5.

The preceding simple retrieves set him up for blinds. He half expects something is there.

MOWED PATH...BLIND

Hide some dummies or dead birds at the end of the path. Send the dog from line; the path will lead him to the first blind. Send him back until he has cleaned up all the birds.

We'll do in water what we did on the arm of the "H." Take a line in water just like land.

"MOWED" PATH IN WATER

Throw six dummies in a line down the center of a pond. Let the dog see the assistant throw them out. The nearest one should be about 20 yards, the farthest about 100. Send him just as you did on land.

LINING IN WATER

After he's been doing the mowed path in water without any problems, he's ready to be send on a blind. Do all this water work from the exact spot and in the same direction as the mowed water path. If he pops, call him in and make him start over. If he doesn't get the idea that he's supposed to swim a straight line until told to stop on whistle, have an assistant throw a long single for him down the center of the water.

When he has done this, have the assistant retire or hide. Then send him back to the same area that he has just returned from.

When he gets a good way out and has passed where the assistant is hiding on shore, have the assistant throw a dummy ahead of the dog.

He'll soon get the idea that you want him to line in water just as he does on land. Now the sending arm signal will come to mean what it's supposed to mean: a direction.

When he does this, it's quite an accomplishment. Give him a lot of

This is an open body of water. Nothing is in sight. Tar is only a year and a half, but he already believes in me. If I set him up and point the way he knows somehow a bird will be out there to retrieve. Here is how we taught this to him. It is the old incentive game.

1.
Set him up and send him off. If he does not take a straight line call him back. Tell him how stupid he is. Show him you are not pleased, that he better pay attention. Send him off.

praise for this. Then go back to the water path with the dummies just to be sure he has the idea.

Now he's ready to try this in new directions. If he falters, go back to the water path. When you can send him in any direction through the water, you're ready for the next step. Plant a blind across the water; don't make it too long. Next plant the blind across the water and up on the land a short distance. O.K., he has this much, but don't rush to extend him too far. Let time be that teacher.

2.
This time if he gets a good distance out have an assistant throw a dummy out ahead of him.

3.
In short order you can get him to swim to China. Be sure he does not see the assistant. Now give him short blinds so he'll learn the splash isn't what he's looking for, it's the bird.

On blind retrieves the dog may have over-run the fall. We don't want him to think that... ...this COME IN whistle is only used when he needs correction. Throughout the training we...

COME IN BY WHISTLE AND RETRIEVE

You've used the COME-IN whistle to make corrections when he did wrong and you wanted him to start over. You may note that he may start to respond slowly to this command. If so, take him back to his ABC's. On walks command SIT. Then you walk off 75 yards and turn and face him. Make him wait a long time; work up his desire to come to you. Then hit the whistle. Give him praise when he rushes in.

If on a retrieve he defies the whistle, first make sure he's not confused. Make sure he could hear it. If you think he did, get to him pronto. Drag him roughly back to where the whistle was first blown. Raise hell and then make him go through the desired command.

If he develops the piddling habit on returning from a retrieve, give him a rousing NO . . . NO . . . Hit the COME-IN whistle with gusto.

If a dog develops the habit of piddling when on the way to a dummy, stop using dummies and go to birds. The live bird will add the enthusiasm to the retrieve to make him wait with his problem.

...use the COME IN whistle command and give some incentive for obeying, a retrieve. He...

...must learn that just like all other commands this one also can lead him to a bird.

The setup is simple. Start in open cover. Sit him. Throw dummy in close. Whistle him...

...in. Then do it in heavier cover and have a dead bird planted between you and the dog.

Sit him at the crossbar of the "H." Let him see the dummies. You walk down the long...

OVER BY PATH

The center bar in the H is now used. Start by sitting the dog at the 90-degree angle. Walk back down the path. Send the dog over. Since he sees the dummies and the path leads to them, he'll get the idea. Now, when he brings the first one to you, send him from line down the path. Stop him at the H bar; he'll turn and sit, awaiting instructions. Send him over. Now he knows what you want.

Take him to low cover; do the same thing without the paths. Then try him in short blinds . . . remember, short.

Mix the commands up, OVER to the right, OVER to the left.

Some trainers go to great extremes on these hand signals. Their dogs respond to BACK and OVER, not just to the 90-degree angles of these commands, but to the 45-degree angles. The hand directly overhead means straight back. Right arm at the two-o'clock position means back 45 degrees to the right. Left arm raised to the ten-o'clock position means 45 degrees back to the left. The arm at four o'clock combined with the COME-IN whistle means come in 45 degrees to the right, and eight o'clock means to the left. The COME-IN whistle means straight in. This precision is not really necessary for the hunting dog.

... arm of the "H." Give him one whistle blast for attention and the hand signal for over. He has to know what you mean. Give him the release whistle command, two fast blasts and off he goes. He will bring the dummy to you. Set him up at heel. Direct him down the path again. Release him with the two whistle blasts and when he runs and reaches the crossbar of the "H," blast once and stop him. He will sit and face you. Give the cast hand signal. He knows you put more than one there. We try to extend the over cast by having the dummies farther down the line. Next, plant a dead bird and send him over. The next two pages show how we use the arm of the "H" to teach the command BACK. Once he has this, the big "H" can be used for all combinations from all directions. Put blinds out in different spots. Work him from one end of a long arm of the "H." Send him three-quarters of the way down the arm for a blind. Next, send him as far as the crossbar. Stop him. Send him over with the hand signal and the whistle. Have a blind bird planted at the end of that "over" path. Maybe next send him to the end of the long arm. When he returns, send him from heel to the crossbar. Send him over. Stop him where that path meets the other long arm of the "H." Now send him back. Hand signal, hand straight over head. Don't whistle — release him until you think he understands. If he goofs hit him immediately with one blast. Stop him, start over. The paths help him learn what you want.

1. Walk him down the path.

2. Sit him. Walk on, dropping dummies.

BACK...BY PATH

When he brings in first one, send him off.

Stop him with the whistle. Send him back.

166

3. Get his attention. Show him the signal.

Send him off with arm motion and whistle.

He knows the dummies are there, the path... ...directs him, giving your signals meaning.

167

THE DOUBLE "T"

T comes after H. After he has learned basic handling on the moved paths, try this double T. About sixteen dummies are needed. The picture to the left shows the setup. For picture purposes we haven't spread the two arms of the T as wide as they should be. Two dummies are placed at the end of each crossbar. The rest are straight back, a good way.

These pictures and those on the next page show how the game is played. Start this in low cover so he can see what you want him to do. Then try this lesson in heavier cover. Mix them up. Make him have to depend on you for the direction he's to go in.

When you spread these out in heavy cover, take advantage of the wind and the terrain when you give him his side casts. If some of the dummies are across sloping terrain, remember a dog has a tendency to run downhill.

If he gets confused go out and help him. Shorten up your distance between you and the dog. Make him go through with the retrieve. Then increase the distance again; go back to your original position and repeat the command.

Make sure in all these handling lessons that you're wearing light-colored

What we have taught him on the path we transfer to the open field. The cover should hide the dummies after he learns on a lawn to retrieve in the order you select for him. Left is the setup so you can see. Right, send him BACK, a long one. When the whistle release is given, we can also shout BACK immediately as he gets off. This is his signal that it's a long way you want him to go. Turn the page and you'll see more on the double "T."

clothes so you don't blend in with the background. He can't follow your signals if he can't see you.

If you can do this double T with your dog, you have a dog to be proud of; and you, too, can be pretty proud of your work. You're going to hunt with very few hunters who have this much control over their dogs.

Any training you'll do from here on will be fine finishing touches. Tar, in these double-T pictures, was only sixteen months old when these pictures were taken. And he could do this job before that time.

He was sent deep for the last retrieve. Now send him back again, same area. He knows more birds are there. But stop him deep, give him an OVER cast. If he believes you, he'll go.

One last word. Jock and Tar are house pets . . . no, I should really say members of the family. Their job is to be good citizens, and their fun is to go hunting. These dogs went to school on weekends and nights, since I had to go to work in the big city in order to feed them. The point I make is . . . with a logical training system and the new knowledge we now have about dogs, anyone, in short order, can train a retriever for hunting on land or water.

Send him out again. Stop him and give the BACK command. If he starts to think he can do this on his own and doesn't stop immediately on the whistle blast, run out and shake him up.

Next, send him BACK again but stop him short, in line with the close-in pairs. Give him the other side cast. From now on mix them up and make him learn to follow you. Next time you play the double "T" game spread the arms wider. Eventually a side cast means go in that direction till you hear the whistle blast for stop. There is a lot of reward in this game.

RUNNING THE BANK

Often in duck hunting when a bird is down but only winged it will make for the near shore to hide. Here is where the retriever earns his keep. We have tried to keep him from running the bank under certain conditions but here we teach him to search out a cripple. We have placed four dummies on the far bank. At first when we do this he can see them. Later, we'll make them blinds for him.

We head him toward the first one...

...When he gets there, blast STOP. Give...

...him an OVER cast, he'll run, pick up, return..

...he may be getting the idea...

...Back he's sent to the original spot...

...He's sent and returns...

...Now, we send him back to the same spot...

..He's brought in two. Send him back to same spot...

...Now it's a longer run of the bank...

...We've stopped him as he hits land and...

...sent him OVER to find the last one.

REVERSE THE DOUBLE

Often in hunting, two birds will be dropped on one pass. One bird, the second one down, could be as dead as a duck. The first, let's say, was a cripple. The dog naturally will go for the last bird down first. But in this case we'll want him to go for the cripple first so it won't get away, the other one later. If he goofs on this call him back, start him over. The key here is to change his position. Get his mind off that second bird.

Throw a dummy, let it splash...

...Throw second one closer, splash it...

...Command NO! NO! Make it stick...

174

...Heel him. Move him, this won't be...

...necessary later. Face him to the first...

...bird. Send him. Second bird is still there. We've all the time in the world to get that one.

IGNORE IT — GO FOR THE BLIND

The next step after the preceding lesson is again useful in hunting. Here we call him off an obvious dead bird and send him for a blind that he didn't see down or a duck that is floating away on the tide. The procedure is the same. We show him the splash. Command NO! NO! Move him to get his mind oriented off that bird and onto the business at hand. Set him up pointing him toward the blind, (pictures left). Note the top of page 177, he looks over at the floating dummy, but goes on with his line. Up he goes on the bank, following his line. The white speck is the dummy. He finds the land blind, mission is completed.

MISSION COMPLETED

With that blind, Tar's mission is completed, so is mine. We've tried to give you all the high points. We've tried to give you some information on how to tackle the problems of training a retriever. Sure we have missed some things. For example, if your dog creeps on line out of sheer excitement, we expect you to figure out how to handle it. Give him a good slap on the sitting end and demand that he sit at heel. He'll heel. Also, we haven't talked much about triples. Two and one is three and that's how you make them, after you're sure your dog understands two.

Another thing we have not mentioned. If you have the problem of a dog whining on line or crying after he leaves line, just out of sheer excitement . . . don't ask me how to cure it.

I've never figured that one out s of removing his squawk box.

We have not given you a precise time schedule step by step. We have only tried to approximate the schedule for you. Use your head, watch your dog, and you can figure that one out.

We haven't said much about a dog spooking people or things. We've brought him up so that we don't expect this problem. If he does get frightened by a situation, and even secure people can be frightened, lay off training for a day or so. Then work him back slowly into the same situation.

You're going to get a lot of fun out of training, and a lot of work. Sure we have asked a lot of the dog, too. Maybe more than other folks have asked in the past. Tar was only twenty months old when the pictures on this page were taken. That doesn't mean he's graduated. He still needs all kinds of experiences in all kinds of cover and conditions to learn. He does know what's expected and he does know I know what he can do. We pushed him as far and as fast as he would accept it. But remember something that was said before. If a retriever can be a guide dog with the responsibility of someone's life at the age of a year and a half, we should expect that our retrievers can do a full competent job in the same period of time. Try it and see.

INDEX